Praise for *Designing the Conversation*

A book on facilitation? I wouldn't have thought this was needed, but after reading Designing the Conversation, *I'm reminded of all the valuable skills we learn—with some difficulty, mind you—on our own. Fortunately, all that stuff is covered here, from preparing for a session to handling the difficult personalities. And it's all delivered in a way that's short, to the point, and packed with plenty of pop culture references, making this a fun, lively read! You'll grin at uncomfortably familiar situations and nod in agreement as bits of invaluable advice are served in style through every chapter.*

Stephen P. Anderson,
Independent Consultant and Author of Seductive Interaction Design

As a user experience professional, you know how to get inside your users' heads to understand their mindset, needs, and goals. Those same skills can help you communicate more effectively with your colleagues, clients, bosses—even strangers. This book taps into the collective wisdom of dozens of experts, showing you how to engage and facilitate more meaningful discussions.

Karen McGrane, Managing Partner, Bond Art + Science,
and author, Content Strategy for Mobile (A Book Apart, 2012)

If you spend any time speaking with users, stakeholders, and any other people, you need to read Designing the Conversation: Techniques for Successful Facilitation. *Within a few short chapters I was completely rethinking my process in how to best reach, and utilize, quality user and stakeholder feedback.*

Shay Howe, Designer and Front-End Developer, The Starter League

This comprehensive, handy, easy-to-read guide is full of tips, tricks, and techniques that will soon have you facilitating like a pro.

Dave Gray, consultant, facilitator,
and coauthor of Gamestorming: A Playbook for Innovators,
Rulebreakers, and Changemakers

In the design field, we work with a wide variety of team members while building products. It is not uncommon for communication hurdles to arise during the product design process. Communication, collaboration, and facilitation skills are key to improving the conversations around design. Designing the Conversation: Techniques for Successful Facilitation *provides valuable, practical insights that are useful for sharpening facilitation skills and improving the conversations had with stakeholders, team members, and, of course, users.*

Aaron Irizarry, Experience Designer, Hewlett-Packard

Praise for *Designing the Conversation*

This is a special book. With Designing the Conversation, *Unger, Nunnally, and Willis have written the definitive guide to practical, accessible facilitation. There's no jargon or mind-numbing filler here, just an excellent balance of theory, technique, and practical, real-world examples. It's an excellent addition to any designer's daily toolbox.*

Matthew Milan, Partner, Normative

Chock-full of useful and thought-provoking quotes by everyone from Voltaire and the Indigo Girls to Seinfeld, Chinese proverbs, and contemporary facilitation experts, Designing the Conversation *is a great resource for anyone who aspires to bring their wit, wisdom, and knowledge to the podium. Russ Unger, Brad Nunnally, and Dan Willis cover in great detail all the potential opportunities and pitfalls that can arise when facilitating workshops and presentations, offering sound advice for overcoming hurdles and best practices for making your audience's experience the best it can possibly be.*

**Tim Frick, speaker, author of Return on Engagement:
Content, Strategy, and Design Techniques for Digital Marketing,
and owner of Mightybytes, a Chicago-based web design and digital marketing firm**

If you can't talk to your clients and customers, you can't make great products. Every young designer and product manager should read this book; the good stuff they forgot to teach you in school is laid out in these pages in clear, readable, and playful prose.

Christina Wodtke, Publisher, Boxes and Arrows

The discipline of design may be about users and interfaces, but the practice *of design is about facilitation. Dan, Brad, and Russ have written a clear, concise handbook packed with tips, insights, and years of experience. Designers—and an entire consulting industry— can use this book to make sure every meeting, workshop, presentation, or working session you ever schedule goes off like a charm.*

Austin Govella, Experience Design Manager, Avanade

Buy this book. Then read it. Then read it again. Projects that fail don't fail because of poor technology choices, bad design, or evil clients. They fail because the people working on them are pulling in different directions. Designing the Conversation *will teach you how to start a conversation with everyone involved with your project. Facilitating a conversation with your stakeholders won't guarantee success. But failing to do so will guarantee failure.*

Rich Quick, Head Web Developer, Arnold Clark Automobiles, Scotland, UK

Designing the Conversation

Techniques for Successful Facilitation

Russ Unger   Brad Nunnally   Dan Willis

New Riders   VOICES THAT MATTER™

Designing the Conversation: Techniques for Successful Facilitation
Russ Unger, Dan Willis, and Brad Nunnally

New Riders
www.newriders.com

New Riders is an imprint of Peachpit, a division of Pearson Education

Find us on the Web at www.newriders.com
To report errors, please send a note to errata@peachpit.com

Acquisitions Editor: Michael Nolan
Project Editor: Valerie Witte
Production Editor: Katerina Malone
Developmental Editor: Margaret Anderson
Copyeditor: Gretchen Dykstra
Proofreader: Patricia Pane
Composition: Danielle Foster
Indexer: James Minkin
Cover and Interior Design: Mimi Heft
Interior Illustrations: Dan Willis

ISBN-13: 978-0-321-88672-9
ISBN-10: 0-321-88672-0

9 8 7 6 5 4 3 2 1

Printed and bound in the United States of America

Acknowledgments

Russ Unger

There's something about writing a book. I've not birthed a child, so I can't pretend to fathom that experience, but my understanding is that eventually you forget certain things and agree to the idea of having another. What I'm trying to get to is, well, it's something like that. Except this time I roped two other people into doing it with me, and they were exceptional people to do anything with, and extremely so in this undertaking.

My wife, Nicolle, and our daughters, Sydney and Avery, were extremely supportive, and I am proud and grateful for love, laughter, and space that they gave me when it was needed; you make it all worthwhile. My mother is an incredible woman who has always been supportive of me, and while we were writing this book, it became my turn to return the favor. A lot of my world turned upside down as hers did, which didn't always make me the most fun person to be around. Yet, we're all here today, and that's a pretty good outcome.

Brad and Dan made me a better writer, and they made me constantly excited by what they were writing, and that's such a blessing. If you haven't already flipped through the pages of this book to look at the illustrations that Dan has created, you should do so. They're nothing short of phenomenal, and they tie in so nicely with our content. Every time a new illustration appeared in our folders, I was consistently amazed and impressed by his talent and creativity. I hope you are, too.

A lot of people helped out along the way, from the various experts who provided timely, intelligent content to the friends who chimed in with support. As always, Brad Simpson (www.i-rradiate.com) was the first round of support in helping me make sure that my design elements were sharp, crisp, and, of course, following publisher guidelines. Gabby Hon, the late Dr. Arthur P. Doederlein and his *so what?*, Mark Brooks, Stephen Anderson, Jared Spool, Lou Rosenfeld, Laura Creekmore, Eduardo Ortiz, Tim Frick, Dan R. Brown, Fred Beecher, Adam Connor, Matthew Grocki, Steve "Doc" Baty, Christina Wodtke, Nishant Kothary, Shay Howe, Rich Quick, Austin Govella, Matthew Milan, Todd Zaki Warfel, Eduardo Ortiz, Aaron Irizarry, the #SubChiUX gang, and the UXsters all helped out in a bunch of different ways, but mostly by being good friends along the way, and keeping my head straight and my laughter present. The Cranky Talk Workshops for New Speakers faculty and alumni have been a great inspiration in this effort, as well.

The contributors are some of the smartest people I know, and you should type all of these names into your favorite search engine, learn more about them, and follow their work. They made me much smarter through this process, and I'm extremely grateful for their assistance. In no certain order, these brilliant people are Scott Berkun, Christina Wodtke, Samantha Starmer, Dana Chisnell, Luke Wroblewski, Christine Cronin, Richard Dalton, Dan Roam, Nathan Shedroff, Eric L. Reiss, Cennydd Bowles, Andy Budd, Shay Howe, Aaron Irizarry, Brad Smith, Jennifer Jones, David Farkas, Steve "Doc" Baty, Nishant Kothary, Margot Bloomstein, Tim Frick, Fred Beecher, Laura Creekmore, Bill DeRouchey, Nick Disabato, Dale Sande, Ross Belmont, Jared Spool, Chris Risdon, Josie Scott, James Macanufo, Rob Moore, Sunni Brown, Christopher Fahey, Marc Rettig, Jesse James Garrett, Alex Dittmer, C. E. Lane, Eytan Mirsky, Erik Soens, Adam Polansky, Dave Malouf, Kate Niederhoffer, Peter Kim, Donna Spencer, and Jason Kunesh.

And, of course, Jonathan "Yoni" Knoll, if for no other reason than being himself.

All the great folks at New Riders really help make a sometimes bumpy road less so, and I'm thankful that we got to work with Michael Nolan, Glenn Bisignani, Valerie Witte, Gretchen Dykstra, Mimi Heft, Katerina Malone, Patricia Pane, Danielle Foster, James Minkin, and Margaret Anderson.

Finally, it's important to note that without organizations like the Information Architecture Institute, the Interaction Design Association, and others, it would have been impossible for me to make the connections with many of the people mentioned. If you're at all curious about the field of UX design, go explore these organizations, join them, and get involved!

Dan Willis

I want to thank my daughter, who has no idea how much support she gave me, and my wife, who knows exactly how much support she has given me in this and dozens of other crazy-ass projects over the years. Nothing I do would mean anything without Lanie and Eva.

For my work on this book, I depended heavily on the big brains of others. The idea that I can send out a call and get so much great content from so many people humbles me. I'm tempted to list them all here, but then you'd just skim the rest of my acknowledgements and I hate the idea of losing an audience. So instead, I encourage you to hunt down the insights generously supplied by those folks for the chapters I wrote: Brainstorming, Sales Calls, Mentoring, Virtual Seminars, Lectures, and Measuring Success.

I also want to thank everyone involved in any way with the Cranky Talk Workshops for New Speakers, which I've had the pleasure to run the last few years. The energy, knowledge, and continuing support of the faculty and students of those events have changed me in wonderful and unexpected ways. It is an honor to be part of that tiny, yet robust community. Now that this damn book is out of the way, I hope to start scheduling more sessions and we'll see how much we can expand the Cranky Family.

Finally, I want to thank Russ and Brad for the freedom they gave me in illustrating this book. The last time I got that much elbow room on a group project, I was in high school and I botched the execution. Hopefully this time around I've been a bit more successful. There are some weird ideas and plenty of ugly, fat people in my drawings and yet I got nothing but encouragement from my coauthors. They didn't have to do that and I very much appreciate that they did.

Brad Nunnally

It has always been a dream of mine to write a book. When Russ approached me with the idea for this book and told me he wanted Dan to be involved, I saw this dream becoming a reality. I also knew I'd be working with two of the smartest people I know. I've become a better writer and a better person after collaborating with these two gentlemen. The lessons I've learned while writing this book will serve me for years to come. There are no words that can communicate how grateful I am to Russ and Dan for this opportunity.

A special note is necessary about Dan and his illustrations. Dan's illustrations are, in my opinion, the one thing that brings this whole book together. They convey the tone and the spirit of the information you will find and it was truly a gift to see him create such wonderful art.

There are two other people I owe the world to, and they are my loving wife, Kim, and my son, Tristan. I am blessed to have both their presence and their support in my life. The patience my wife has shown me while I worked into the night is a debt I will never be able to fully repay, no matter how many St. Louis Cardinals games I send her to. Even though he is only three years old, Tristan reminded me that sometimes it's necessary to step back and just play and enjoy life. This lesson, more than anything, helped me get past the barriers that pop up during any project one undertakes.

I owe much to my family, especially my mother and father for instilling a love for reading in me at an early age. I'm grateful for my in-laws, especially Ray "Opa" Schneider, who every Sunday at the family dinner asked if the book was done yet.

This simple question kept me focused and it was a good day when I could tell him, "Yes, it's finally done."

My good friend and #UXFrathaus mate David Farkas deserves special thanks for being a voice of reason over IMs, a thorough draft reviewer, and a willing contributor.

My coworkers at Perficient XD deserve special thanks for their patience with me over these last few months and for allowing me to bounce ideas off them. The team I work with is filled with some of the most talented people I know, and it's a pleasure to work with them every day.

I am grateful to my many friends and professional peers within the UX community: Diego Pulido, Eduardo Ortiz, Chris Avore, Gabby Hon, Jared Spool, Lou Rosenfeld, Jeff Parks, Chris Risdon, Adam Polansky, Fred Beecher, Nathan Verrill, Christina Wodtke, David Gray, Chris Baum, Eric L. Reiss, Andrew Hinton, Dan Shipton, and many more who have graciously shared a beer with me, listened to my ideas, and welcomed my thoughts over the years. You all have made me smarter simply by knowing you.

I will forever be in the debt of both Whitney Hess and Jonathan "Yoni" Knoll. I am so lucky to have befriended you all those years ago and your guidance put me on a path that I would never have dreamed possible.

My gratitude for the experts who agreed to contribute to this book—Carol Righi, Kevin Hoffman, Adam Connor, Aaron Irizarry, and Dana Chisnell—is immeasurable.

I learned very quickly that a successful book isn't created solely by the writing team. It takes everyone behind the scenes as well. To the team at New Riders, I'm thankful for all the work you've done in putting this book together, reviewing our drafts, and pushing us to meet our deadlines. Thank you Michael Nolan, Glenn Bisignani, Valerie Witte, Gretchen Dykstra, Mimi Heft, Katerina Malone, Patricia Pane, Danielle Foster, James Minkin, and Margaret Anderson.

I owe much to wonderful organizations like the Information Architecture Institute, the Interaction Design Association, and others. The body of knowledge represented by the members and the connections these organizations have provided to me made my career possible. You won't find more open, friendly, and nurturing people than the ones in the field of UX. I encourage you to join, participate, and contribute so we can all continue to grow.

Finally, I'd like to thank my late father-in-law, Kevin Schneider. He was a second father to me and I wish he could be here to see this book get published and play one last round of gin rummy with the family.

Contents

Introduction

Why we wrote this book

It's difficult to think of a professional role that doesn't have some degree of facilitation attached to it. You may not consider "presenting" or "pitching" or "brainstorming" or "interviewing" to be a part of your job description when you explain what you do. However, this core soft skill—which centers around dealing with and directing people—is at the heart of what many of us do.

We are designers, and as designers, we think about how people interact with the world around them. We love to do research and we love to watch users doing their thing because these are the activities that help us perform the actual design activities that shape our work, which we like to think we're already pretty good at. It takes skill and practice to be able to facilitate people, and facilitation is truly the foundation of an effective design practice. Facilitation skills help us collaborate with and lead others to ensure that their ideas have been heard and have contributed to the design process.

Our goal with *Designing the Conversation* is to give you the basic tools and context to help you facilitate in some of the most common scenarios. As you'll see in many of the chapters, we're not trying to be everything to all people, but we're trying to provide you with the core information and knowledge you'll need to perform many of the facilitation activities you may encounter, not just the ones mentioned in this book. Beyond our own examples, we provide you with the insight and experience of some of the brightest minds in the field.

But, this book isn't just for designers, just because we are. This book is very practical for those in a variety of fields: marketing, product management, business analysts, managers, human resources professionals, and so on.

We hope we've done a decent job of articulating that this is a pretty good starting point for a variety of facilitation types and activities, and more importantly, we hope you think so, too.

Who should read this book

Designing the Conversation provides a broad, introductory overview to facilitation within the context of three main types of facilitation: group facilitation, one-on-one, and one-on-many. Anyone who has an interest in becoming a better facilitator—whether you're a designer, product manager, marketer, or someone who's interested in sharing your knowledge with others—should find something useful between the covers of this book.

We didn't take a "deep dive" approach to the topics highlighted in this book; our goal was to provide you with the knowledge you need to be prepared and to get started facilitating as quickly as possible. In most cases, we've highlighted leading experts and resources that can help you go deep on the subjects you have the most interest in. Mostly, however, we want to help you put this information to good work as quickly as possible.

How to use this book

There are many excellent resources out there about the innumerable types of facilitation. The chapters in this book could each be covered in much deeper detail in books of their own—and in several cases they already have by other talented authors, many of whom we learned from ourselves.

The best way to use this book is to take the following approach:

- **Everyone, well almost everyone,** should read Section 1, "Facilitation Preparation," and Section 5, "Post-Facilitation." In these sections, you'll find invaluable information about how to plan and prepare, be aware of the different factors that can impact your ability to facilitate, and handle everything that can take place when your facilitation activity is complete.

- **The book makes for a great end-to-end read (in our humblest of opinions);** however, once you've read sections one and five, you may find it best to pogo stick around the book to the subjects that interest you most.

- **If group facilitation is your need,** Section 2, "Group Facilitation," is where you want to start. There are chapters on Workshops (7), Brainstorming (8), Focus Groups (9), and Participatory Design (10).

- **If you're facilitating in one-on-one scenarios,** you'll find Section 3, "One-on-One Facilitation," most beneficial. There are chapters that focus on Interviews (11), Usability Testing (12), Sales Calls (13), and Mentoring (14).

- **If you're going to stand in front of a group of people and share information with them,** Section 4, "One-on-Many Facilitation," provides you with chapters on Conference Presentations (15), Virtual Seminars (16), and Lectures (17).

- **Finally, if you're interested in stories from other experts,** Practicing (6) is loaded with information detailing how leaders in their fields practice for facilitation. Horror Stories (20) shares some experts' personal experiences of things gone wrong. Their situations might have felt catastrophic at the time, but now we can all use them to reflect on and laugh about, at least a little, with them. Be sure to visit www.designingtheconversation.com for bonus stories in extended versions of both of these chapters.

Section 1

Facilitation Preparation

Whether you're facilitating with only one other person in the room or more people than you can count, there are some basics you should be familiar with. Being prepared to deal with a variety of content, location, technology, and people issues will help you to become a successful facilitator.

Chapter 1

Preparation

It's time to tie your loose ends up.
—Tommy Stinson

Car salesman: "Looks like we're going to need some gas."

Kramer: "Oh, well how much gas you think is in there right now?"

Car salesman: "Well, it's on E."

Kramer: "You know, oftentimes, Jerry, he lends me his car and I find myself in a situation where the car is almost out of gas. But for a variety of reasons, I don't want to be the one responsible for purchasing costly gasoline."

Car salesman: "So you want to know how far you can drive your friend's car for free?"

In this scene from the series *Seinfeld*, Kramer was attempting to learn how far he could drive a car once the gas gauge gets to E—or beyond. I think if we reflect sincerely, we'd all love to know what "empty" really means in our vehicles, but the context here was clear: Kramer wanted to drive this particular vehicle to empty so he'd know how far he could drive Jerry's car without having to put gas in it.

Kramer wanted to be prepared.

As a facilitator, you should take similar steps to ensure that you're well prepared, too.

Meet the Expert: Scott Berkun

Scott Berkun is the best-selling author of *The Myths of Innovation* (O'Reilly, 2010), *Confessions of a Public Speaker* (O'Reilly, 2011), and *MindFire* (Berkun Media, 2011). He writes a popular blog at www.scottberkun.com and tweets at @berkun.

•

I believe in applying UX-type methods to speaking. The goal should be rapid prototyping. Put together a rough outline, and maybe some rough slides, and then stand up and try to give the talk. Within the first few minutes of practicing, I quickly find things that I need to change, and I go and change them and then start practicing, from the beginning, again. I keep going until I can make it through the entire talk without changing anything.

This process builds the talk based on how it flows. It makes it immediately obvious when a slide or a point doesn't fit with the previous slide or point, and lets me correct it early on. It also ensures that the first five or ten minutes of the talk will have been practiced and refined many times before I ever give it to an audience.

When we discuss preparation, you need to realize that, as the facilitator, you truly are presenting. You have a plan, you have a topic, and you're directing the story. And even though you may not always be doing all the work, you are **orchestrating** it, and that is hard, hard work.

What is it about good stories that make it easy to follow the plot without getting lost, confused, or chasing down the backstory of irrelevant characters? Good stories make it easy to suspend disbelief and jump right into the scenes without looking back—but sometimes there's a disconnect that sends the audience back into their seats trying to figure out what happened.

It turns out that behind every good story is a well-planned, well-prepared, logical structure and narrative flow. It turns out that properly planned and prepared facilitation can also keep audiences tuned in and focused, too.

Project facilitation activities, as they appear in this book, are not much different. With proper planning, you can pull together all kinds of information from various sources and structure it to formulate a story—or stories—and a flow that helps you communicate your information in a way that makes sense to your audience.

This approach to public speaking can apply to how you tackle your project facilitation plan and to how you prepare to present the materials to your audience. Regardless of your method, the structure and flow of your activity will help keep your audience on track, keep them in the flow, and lead them to a final plot point where all the information they've received comes to a nicely tied together outcome.

It's all part of the plan

Once you've nailed down the topic of your facilitation, you'll likely set off on a journey of research that will help you support your claims. If you happen to be the resident expert on a topic, you may need to do a brain dump to get the information out of your head and onto paper.

You see, this information is awesome. However, the problem with information is that the more you have, the more difficult it is to keep it all straight. And if you can't keep it all straight, how can you expect your audience to follow along? This, of course, is where proper planning comes into play.

Christina Wodtke, author of *Information Architecture: Blueprints for the Web* (New Riders, 2009) and publisher of the design journal *Boxes and Arrows* (www.boxesandarrows.com), says:

> **First draft:** Say everything quickly.
>
> **Second draft:** Replace pronouns with nouns, explain anything that's vague.
>
> **Third draft:** Omit needless words.
>
> **Fourth draft:** Get the music of the prose right.

The big takeaway is to get all your ideas out first. Let them flow without reservation so you can have a full view of the information playing field. Then, you can turn that into something coherent.

A brain dump can consist of keywords, phrases, full sentences, paragraphs, sketches, photos—as little or as much as you need to help shape your content. Jim Henson, the creator of the Muppets, used to carry a little red book around with him. His red book contained all his ideas, and included every type of content previously mentioned. When you're trying to take your ideas from the raw format to something more tangible and better structured, find your own little red book, such as a dedicated whiteboard, a sketch/notepad or Moleskine, or your favorite digital tool.

Once you get all the little bits out of that fascinating mind of yours, you can start to refine them and turn them into something that will make sense to your audience.

Meet the Expert: Samantha Starmer

Samantha Starmer, a faculty member of the Cranky Talk Workshops (http://crankytalk.com), focuses on structuring a presentation.

•

Start with your big idea. What is The One Thing that you want your audience to remember after you're done with your presentation or facilitated activity? Hone in on that one thing with a laser focus and make sure that all the work you do ties back to it.

Next, define the story—make sure you have coherently established a beginning, a middle, and, of course, an ending that ties everything together nicely. Everything has to point back to the one thing you defined previously! As you go through defining your story, be aware not only of who your audience is, but also how you would explain it to someone who has a lot less background on the topic than you, such as a grandmother or a child.

Be aware of your style—some presenters are active and make full gestures, others stand calmly at the podium, and some even ad-lib and interject funny, personal stories. Discover your own style, but don't force yourself to fit into someone else's mold; be natural and be yourself. The best way to uncover this is to find a willing audience and practice, practice, practice. Collect a lot of feedback and be open to it; the audience will want you to succeed!

If you find that you're particularly nervous or uncomfortable, more structure will help you alleviate this fear, unless you're incredibly awesome at improv, in which case you probably wouldn't be reading along!

When you're structuring your presentation or facilitation exercise, remember to build to the amount of time you're allotted. The challenge is to understand how much information you can fit into the time slot; it's always better to fall a little short than to go over, and you can spend additional time on questions and answers with the audience in those cases. How much time do you need? For some, it's one minute for one slide; for others, it's one point for five minutes. You have to work this out for yourself, and that will take time. Practice, revise, practice again, and eventually the concept of content to time will have a meaning specific to you.

Remember to work without constraints when you first begin to structure your presentation. Let all the information out, and then, let it rest. Throw away the ideas that aren't working and let the new ideas get added as you uncover them. Estimate the amount of time you'll need to prepare and then double it, especially when working on new material! Don't be shy about getting down and dirty with paper prototypes and testing out your material. Continue to iterate until you're comfortable enough to sit down in front of your presentation tool and crank out whatever slides or materials you need.

Be sure to stay true to your story and keep your narrative as your North Star. Throw out any extraneous information and materials, no matter how cool they might be. If they're not needed or relevant, cut them mercilessly.

Oh, and don't forget: Have fun!

Structure can be daunting; it forces you take the jumble of information that came out of your brain and turn it into easily digestible content that contains solid nuggets of your knowledge and wisdom.

Starmer's advice on structure is sound direction for any type of facilitation activity. Remember, there are many different approaches to planning and structuring content. What works for one person may not work for you at all. Some people may take an aggressive, iterative approach to creating content and others may start by writing in essay format because that's what works for them.

Meet the Expert: Luke Wroblewski

Luke Wroblewski is an internationally recognized digital product leader who has designed or contributed to software used by more than 700 million people worldwide. He is the author of *Web Form Design* (Rosenfeld, 2008) and *Mobile First* (A Book Apart, 2011).

•

1. I make like Pooh Bear and "think, think, think." There's a long period of time where I'm just stewing ideas before I ever write anything down. This usually takes weeks if not months. I've got a concept/goal I'm working on and I just let it percolate as I do other stuff. Occasionally, I'll make a few quick notes if I get inspired, but nothing formal. I also go mountain biking at least once a week and bring a digital voice recorder with me. When climbing for an hour up a mountain, my mind goes blank and ideas come to me. I huff and puff into the recorder to capture the little flashes of insight I get. It sounds awful on the recording, but getting out regularly like this really has given me some of my clearest thinking ever.

2. I make an outline. Whether it's a talk or a book or an article, I make a quick (often detailed) outline of the points I want to convey. For *Mobile First* I made a twenty-five-page outline for a hundred-page book. It was literally *all* the points I wanted to make in the book; it wasn't well organized, just loosely put together, but most of it was there.

3. I start making slides or writing paragraphs/chapters or whatever the medium is. I tend to cross off things in the outline as I add them to the "final artifact." This is to create raw materials that I can then move around as I firm up the story.

4. I start to work on the narrative. I rearrange slides/chapters until there's a coherent story. Sometimes things get added and/or trimmed, but at this point I'm aiming for a unifying arc, a cohesion to all the bits and pieces I assembled. I do this best when I have all the bits and pieces kind of complete, such as complete slides that I can move around to fit the story.

5. I either read it over and over or present it over and over again, refining it based on the feeling and reactions I get. This is a never-ending process—I keep adapting/tweaking until the material runs its course. This can sometimes take years.

Everyone has learned and finessed their approach to preparing and planning mostly by going through facilitation experiences and receiving feedback, critiques, or even watching themselves on video. There's no one-size-fits-all approach to planning and preparation, so don't look for something to be prescriptive; instead look for the parts that make sense to you and that fit into your own approach.

Over time, you'll identify an approach to planning that works for you. Many people who present and facilitate find that the planning, structuring, preparation, and practicing phases all start to blend together.

If you're new to presenting and facilitating, start simple. Gather your thoughts, create an outline, add details and refine, and then think about creating presentation materials (like note cards or slides) to reinforce your structure. Find a friend who's a good listener, or a family member who owes you a favor, and assess whether they end up with an understanding of the topic. That process can help you further improve your content for primetime.

So what?

After you've completed your planning and wrapped up everything in a nice package that highlights the key points of your content, you may think you're done. But there's one more question: So what?

The late Dr. Arthur P. Doederlein, a highly regarded and respected professor at Northern Illinois University, was known for torturing his students with a dreaded *so what* portion of the work that was expected of them. The *so what* was an approach that Dr. Doederlein believed would help his students not just turn in pat answers, but instead challenge them to provide a rationale that explained how—and why—a solution was achieved.

Meet the Expert: Christine Cronin

Christine Cronin is a member of the adjunct faculty in communications at Waubonsee Community College in Sugar Grove, Illinois. She currently teaches courses in public speaking and interpersonal communication.

•

So what? Two simple, innocuous words that mean, well, *everything.* When Dr. Doederlein used to ask us to explain ourselves with the *so what* question, he was challenging us to take our learning a step further. Previous to his course, all of my education had been fairly simple memorization and application. Requiring us to answer *so what* pushed us to not only understand the material, but also relate it to the larger picture. So what does this all mean, whether that be additional concepts in the course or our lives themselves.

Dr. Doederlein believed in being authentic above all else—authenticity in thinking, behavior, and the very choices we make in our lives. So there was never any fluff to his course; if we were studying it, there was a reason. And his requirement—our challenge—was to divine the reason behind the lesson and decide its meaning in our lives. So what?

As a college instructor myself, *so what* now appears in my classroom every day. I still feel Dr. Doederlein's call for that answer, and I challenge myself to make sure all that I teach my students is authentic and relevant. But I also require the *so what* of them. Their academic careers may also be filled with memorization and regurgitation, but for the sixteen weeks that I get to interact with them, I try to continue that legacy of challenging my students to think—truly think—and decide for themselves "so what does this all mean to me?"

At the heart of any prepared content, ask yourself, *so what?* Why should your audience care? Be authentic when you answer, and relate it all to the bigger picture so you're not leaving any spaces unexplored or unaccounted for.

Chapter 2

Define the Whys

Daddy, why is the sky blue?

They seemed like simple questions when we were children, so we asked them all the time. Fascinated by the world around us, we were driven to understand the inner workings of anything our young eyes beheld. Why is the sky blue? Why do butterflies have such pretty wings? Why do we have to wash our hands before we eat dinner?

The need to understand is baked into our DNA. It sent almost five hundred humans into outer space during the second half of the twentieth century and, in this century, it helped scientists create bacteria that can be programmed like a computer. It all started, and will always start with, someone asking *why*.

Unleash your inner child

We encourage children's curiosity and try our best to weather the barrage of questions that results. But as a child matures, those questions start to feel more annoying than charming. It's not surprising that many adults suppress the desire to ask *why*. It might be fine for rocket scientists and synthetic biologists to constantly question what they observe, but in ordinary conversation, it just seems rude. And that's a real shame.

Why has a place in the adult world for the same reason it belonged in our childhood. It's an expression of curiosity and the drive toward understanding. It quickly, and effortlessly, cuts through all the distractions and layers of bureaucracy that bogs so many people down both in life and in business.

Knowing when to ask *why* and where to direct the question is a key facilitation skill. A practiced facilitator will set aside the fear of breaching etiquette and reignite curiosity and the childhood love of asking simple questions that have complicated answers.

Ask the right person in a meeting *why* and you unleash the entire group's energy for investigating the core issues of a topic. It converts the conversation into a learning opportunity where any issue can be deconstructed to its elements and then rebuilt with a common understanding shared by all participants.

A facilitator is also able to guide participants into regulating their own group dynamics with a well-placed *why*. Some topics can do more harm than good if left to be discussed unchecked. Allowing participants to determine the value and level of interest for themselves keeps the troublemaking topic at bay and helps maintain the overall flow of the conversation.

Novice facilitators often overuse the *why* question in the beginning. It's important to use this tool only when necessary and only when it serves a well-planned-out purpose.

Unearth the underlying *why*

Simply asking *why* in a meeting is rarely ever enough to gain an understanding of complex problems. A facilitator can use a series of smaller questions to help participants address larger problems. The success of these questions hinges on both the tone and discretion of the facilitator. Emphasizing the appropriate word, or pausing at the right moment, is essential to turning a question that would normally put a participant on the defensive into a situation where she opens up and delivers insightful information. For example, consider the difference between "Why is X important?" and "Now, why is that important to X? How does that make it more valuable?"

Why is X important?

This question can help when someone brings up off-topic information. This can happen when a participant gets distracted because a solution fascinates her, but isn't germane to the current conversation. Also, a participant will occasionally introduce a roadblock that shuts down a conversation. In either case, when you question the information's importance, this question forces the participant to make the connection between the information she's introduced and the conversation at hand.

Why does that matter to...?

This question introduces value to the conversation and is best directed to the participants. If the participants assign a high value to an idea, the idea may greatly expand the conversation. If the participants don't see the value, the idea can be comfortably set aside. This tactic allows you to remain neutral while garnering the group's support for high-value ideas. Ending this question with "matter" can be dangerous; you should always tie it back to the topic at hand to avoid coming across as overly aggressive. Why does this matter in terms of the success of our project? Why does this matter with respect to the decision we are trying to make? Tying in the current topic also encourages participants to focus and dive deeper, which can uncover additional discussion points.

Can you explain that to me?

This question can couch an issue in a nonthreatening way, framed as an opportunity for a participant to help you. When the participant then articulates her point, it might provide enough background for another member of the team to support and expand the idea. Or, it might make the idea's weakness clear without requiring you as the facilitator to publicly condemn it.

Is there another way to think about this?

It can be useful to consider the opposite of an idea under consideration by the participants. This tactic helps expose missing aspects of an idea. This question can put any intentionally ignored aspects on clear display.

Did I hear you say...?

A useful tactic for a facilitator is to repeat what a participant says in her own words and with her own filters added. Repeating what was said, either verbatim or slightly rephrased, can help the team reconsider the idea's connection to other points and help the team catch details they may have missed in the heat of discussion. Hearing her own words repeated back to her can help a participant decide whether what she shared really was correct or if she simply spoke up in the heat of the moment.

Typical *why* moments

How does a facilitator know when it's appropriate to pull out one of the above *why* questions? There are signs both before and during a session that indicate when it is OK. The following situations typically come up during a session, and if you performed enough upfront research they can be planned for in the formal agenda.

Situation 1—New Idea

Participant A: *"We could install kiosks at all the office entry points for employees and visitors!"*

Facilitator: *"Why would employees and visitors need a kiosk?"*

Participant B: *"We have employees that travel to different offices all the time; sometimes they need to find someone or somewhere in an office they haven't visited before."*

Participant C: *"Visitors could use them for the same reason, but they shouldn't see the same level of information as an employee."*

Situation 2—Past Roadblock

Participant A: *"Customers accessing the site on their mobile devices won't be able to see that information."*

Facilitator: *"Why can desktop users see it but mobile users can't?"*

Participant A: *"The server the data lives on doesn't have any web services that the mobile platform can access."*

Participant B: *"Yeah, but we could build one, couldn't we?"*

Participant A: *"Yes, it'll just take some time. We'll need to make sure it's part of the plan then."*

Situation 3—Unexpected Discovery

Participant: *"I have this notebook that I use to track all of my out-of-town spending."*

Facilitator: *"Why just your out-of-town spending?"*

Participant: *"Most of the time I travel, it's for work. It's easier come tax time if I track those expenses separately."*

When to ask *why*

Journeys into the *why* take time, so it's important to plan for such excursions whenever possible. You can frequently identify which topics will be particularly contentious or where some set of information is not well understood by the participants. You can predict when these deeper discussions will need to take place and plan your agenda accordingly.

Throughout a session, using *why* lets a topic breathe a bit. It can help the participants gain perspective on a subject. After they've fully explored the topic, you can then steer them back to the larger conversation so they can continue making progress on the agenda.

Sometimes, opportunities to ask *why* appear unexpectedly. That's not a bad thing, as long as they're managed correctly. It can be useful to let the participants drop into a conversational rabbit hole. A confident facilitator will first encourage the distraction and then, at some point, make the decision to steer the participants back to the original topic.

Using *why* with groups vs. solo facilitation

The use of *why* differs when working with a number of participants versus interviewing a single participant.

Group facilitation

Using *why* is a means of gaining a better understanding of a participant's statement or idea. Also, it can help direct the flow of the conversation over time. *Why* is a tool used for both control and exploration.

One-on-one facilitation

The conversation and outcome of sessions that involve just you and a single participant always differ from session to session. New topics, behaviors, or ideas surface as you interview each new person. Using *why* during these times encourages the participant to follow the occasional rabbit hole a bit more freely, and shows her that you are actively listening and that you care.

Climbing out of a rabbit hole

Jumping into a rabbit hole seems like it might be fun: A discussion can run suddenly and deeply in a very specific direction—following what might or might not be a rabbit. You know it's a rabbit hole when it turns out that this pursuit does not lead anywhere. The discussion might trigger new insights, but, as promising as it might seem on the surface, it turns out to be of minimal value. Participants who follow a *why* into a rabbit hole can be pulled back out using the same tactic. You can use *why* to help the participants assess the value of the rabbit hole discussion and its relevance to the group's overall goals.

Getting out of a rabbit hole that doesn't produce anything.

An overly aggressive facilitator may not have the patience required for the participants to decide for themselves that they need to climb out of a hole, but forcing them in a more direct way risks disrupting their energy. Using *why* tends to make for smoother returns, costing time, but not sacrificing the group's sense of progress and self-determination.

Why does *why* matter?

Using *why* throughout a facilitated session and using it appropriately ensures that problem areas are thoroughly explored and participants gain a shared understanding. You can make certain that this happens by asking the participants to explain the value of their overall conversation at the end of a session. The easiest way to do this is to have the participants provide a recap of the discussion, identifying key items and their specific value to the overall project. Using *why* once again as the session is wrapping up lets you capture this shared understanding and determine any necessary next steps.

How do you capture the participants' overall understanding?

- Summarize participants' words on a whiteboard or poster sticky note.
- Distribute a survey for the participants to fill out.
- Have participants rate and sort the major ideas.

When you recap the most important concepts, suggestions, and problems in a session, it encourages self-reflection among participants and provides a sense of completeness for their efforts. It also gives you plenty to work on when it comes to analyzing the information gathered during the session. Mastering *why* is essential for any novice facilitator who wants to get the most out of her sessions going forward.

Chapter 3

Set the Agenda

All best laid plans of mice and men...

— Robert Burns

The agenda is the secret weapon of great facilitators. A well-planned agenda can be the savior that keeps a facilitator on track and on task, and it often provides guidance back to your path when things go off track.

The agenda is a facilitator's secret weapon and most trusted ally. It will save you in times of need, and help wrangle in those that try to go off on their own.

Let's talk about agendas, baby

As a facilitator, creating, setting, and managing an agenda will be one of your primary responsibilities. An agenda may seem so simple that it takes only a few minutes to create and distribute; however, it's often overlooked or, in many cases, ignored by both the facilitator and the participants.

Consider this very common scenario: You walk into a conference room to attend a session without having a clue as to the goals or objectives for the session, who is going to speak when, or who is in charge of the session. At best, this situation is daunting. At worst, it's an absolute debacle of disorganization that puts all parties on the defensive and makes them feel vulnerable.

Yes, this happens every. single. day.

Oh, and you are probably just as guilty yourself.

A session without an agenda is a bagel without cream cheese (or lox, if that's your thing) or a WikiLeaks without a Julian Assange.

Members of the mystery session.

Agendas! What are they good for?

Why does this situation occur? If we take a step back through the process, we can identify two possible faults: not enough time or not enough thinking. When the participants in a session are given a brief understanding of the session's purpose and objectives, it's much easier for them to show up prepared and in the proper frame of mind. When left guessing, they may skew their thinking toward negative thoughts about the session, and as the facilitator you're already behind the eight ball.

And that, friends, is a good enough reason to ensure that there is an agenda in place.

Do not freak out! An agenda is nothing to be afraid of, and in time you'll wonder how you ever worked without one. You may even get to the point where you expect to see an agenda prior to accepting a session invite.

Master of the agenda

The owner of the agenda is the owner of the session, and that is the first step toward successfully facilitating a group of people. Your primary task will be to make sure that all invited attendees understand why they are being included, what is expected of them, and what the results of their participation will be. In addition, those who do not attend will have an understanding and an outcome that they can expect. These are all great reasons to take the task of creating an agenda seriously.

Planning your campaign

The general who thoroughly understands the advantages that accompany variation of tactics knows how to handle his troops. —Sun Tzu

Each battle places its own demands on leaders and their troops. The same applies when you facilitate business owners and technical directors through complicated problems. Having a good grasp of the problem yourself is not enough—you have to understand the limits and politics that may exist within the collaborative group itself.

It's easy to approach every problem with the same plan and the same set of activities. This is not only lazy, but it can end up being a huge risk for the project you're involved in. Take the time to mix things up, introduce new concepts, and understand the "battlefield" you'll be walking into. Think of yourself as a general planning for battle and you'll find your facilitation skills improve time and time again.

Eventually, you'll keep with you a library of agenda templates that will serve you for a variety of situations, from a quick status-check meeting to a full-day workshop. These templates not only save you time, but also help you refine your personal process of facilitation. No two people facilitate in the same way, though there are common patterns, but every facilitator learns to own and rely on his or her own agenda.

Finding your inner purpose

Why are agendas needed in the first place? We're all responsible, professional adults who simply want our company or client to be successful. We should just know how to act and collaborate with one another. *Right...*

The agenda serves two main purposes when it comes to facilitation: informing participants about what will be expected of them and telling them the goals of the session. The bottom line is that it provides a structure that all participants can work within. As humans we love structure. One of the key benefits of structure is an identification of constraints. Without constraints being understood, people have a hard time contributing and providing feedback.

Agendas versus outlines

An agenda differs from a session outline in a few key areas. Agendas typically include a defined timetable, which helps set expectations for what topics are going to be covered and for how long. This timetable is key to ensuring that the flow of facilitation is maintained and that every goal of the gathering is met.

An outline focuses on the highlights of an activity, but doesn't get down into the weeds. Similarly, an agenda doesn't point out every little detail, but it should mention the specific content areas and activities that need to be hit over the course of the facilitated session.

Planning the structure of a session up front also creates a level of trust in the facilitator on the part of the participants. More people are likely to show up, which can be a challenge given how full calendars are these days. Participants will arrive knowing that you have a plan for them and will lead them toward a common understanding around a given subject. This avoids the all-too-common situation of having one or more participants attend a session where at the end they feel their time has been wasted. This leads to a lot of frustration, and can give you a bad name for future sessions.

Once you have an agenda crafted, what do you do with it and where do you send it? If you're responsible for inviting the participants, it's best to send the agenda out as part of the invite, and attached for the convenience of others.

Remember, the agenda helps all participants, including the facilitator. Without one, everyone can easily become lost, distracted, and go off topic. Take the time to write out an agenda, and you can avoid all three of these disastrous effects.

Crafting the agenda

Agendas can be very simple, with just a few bullet points, or they can be constructed with detail and a lot of information. When planning your agenda, consider the extent to which you will need to prepare or provide information for your audience.

Defining the agenda

The actual process of creating an agenda is a simple one. It's a matter of posing a few key questions and using the answers to craft the formal agenda.

- Who are the participants? Facilitating a session among a church group is vastly different than facilitating a session with a group of executives. Understanding who participants are at a high level, their objectives, and motivations, and why they need to be included ensures that the overall group is cohesive.

- What is going to be accomplished? Include a one-sentence "mission statement" on why participants are being brought together and why it's beneficial for them to spend time together.

- What will the participants be producing? If the participants will be collaboratively creating something, prepare proper instructions and gather any necessary supplies.

- What will need to be produced afterward to document the session? Occasionally, you'll need to create something based on the information shared and gathered by the participants. A description of this deliverable should be shared, along with what value it will bring.

By answering these four questions, you can create a well thought-out and structured agenda. These may seem like simple questions, but depending on the context of the session that is being planned, it will become clear that additional work may be required once the session is complete. An example of this would be one where, after crafting the agenda, you realize that it will be impossible to cover all the topics in a single session. The fact that follow-up sessions will be necessary is something that needs to be shared with the participants so they can plan their calendars appropriately.

Structuring the agenda

Agendas come in many shapes and sizes, some of which are included later in this chapter as suggested templates. Specific format aside though, most agendas have key areas that need to be filled out.

Introduction

An introduction can be either brief or fairly in-depth. Some things that help the facilitator when writing the introduction are:

- How exposed are the invitees to the project they're being asked to contribute to?
- How long has the project been going on?
- How complex is the overall project?

At the very least, the introduction needs to provide participants with the background necessary to understand what work has already occurred, and what the overall objective of session is.

Attendee list

In many cases, you'll be handed a list of names, and hopefully corresponding roles, to be included in the session. Depending on the size of the organization, people may or may not know one another. Including a person's role with his or her name helps to provide participants with additional context in terms of importance.

If a senior director sees that the chief marketing officer has been invited to the same session, they are more likely to make room in their schedule to attend.

Objectives and goals

Objectives and goals will explain the reason the participants are being invited and why the session is being held. If your plan includes group-based activities, it's best to include high-level instructions on how those activities will be run in the agenda.

For example, consider a session that will include a design studio as part of the agenda. This activity can sound intimidating to the uninitiated. By providing a high-level overview of the activity, you can reduce participants' apprehension about it.

Timetable

The timetable breaks down the session by topic and activity. This is what you will use to keep everyone on task, and to make sure that every topic area gets the necessary attention. Keeping participants on task and on time is an important aspect of facilitating. In many cases you'll have to deal with people who have very busy calendars, and keeping sessions within a defined time slot helps to ensure that participants don't have to sacrifice time for other things to finish the session.

Outcome

Every session should have an identifiable outcome, otherwise it's pointless to spend the time getting people into a room together. By defining what this outcome will be up front, you ensure that the participants understand that their effort will not be wasted.

Not every outcome can be a concrete deliverable or work product—often this will not be the case. The typical outcome of a session will be additional working sessions. This is not a bad thing, as long as it's part of an overall plan. Eventually though, all this effort needs to culminate in something that is of value and actionable.

Follow-up

It's rare for a session to not require some type of follow-up. Additional sessions are common at the beginning of a project, because a problem is hardly ever fully understood after a single session. The need to conduct a one-on-one interview with a particular participant might come up during a session. This possibility needs to be made clear in the agenda, so it won't come as a surprise when you pull someone aside to ask for a private follow-up.

Once a problem area has been thoroughly explored, review sessions need to be scheduled so participants can agree, or disagree, on what was discussed and created during all the sessions.

There isn't much to an agenda after you break it down to its core components. Depending on the context, any given section might require more or less detail, but overall an agenda is something that helps the facilitator understand what needs to be accomplished and informs participants of what will be expected of them.

Templates

Over time, as you facilitate more and more sessions, you will begin to craft a library of agenda templates that will help you streamline your facilitation preparation. Fortunately for us, some rather smart people have agreed to share the templates they use when preparing for their sessions. Keep in mind, these templates work for their creators, and may or may not be exactly what you need. However, the following samples offer a great starting point for you to begin to craft your own library of templates.

Meeting template

The basic requirements for a generic meeting agenda are why the meeting needs to be called, where people need to go or how should they join the meeting remotely, and what will be covered. If these three basic pieces of information are provided, participants show up to the meeting prepared to review a previously made decision or come to an agreement on a new decision (**Figure 3.1**).

Meeting Agenda

Project Status Meeting
November 12, 2012
10:00–11:00 A.M.

Location: The Bean Conference Room
Dial-in Information: 800-123-4567
Attendee Code: 1234567#
Online Conference Location:
http://meeting.yourcompany.com/

Attendees: Herman Munster, Marilyn Munster, Edward Dudley, Clyde Thornton, Yolanda Cribbins, and Elsa Hyde

Meeting Purpose:
- Review the current status on Research, Graphic Design and SEO
- Discuss outstanding issues
- Prioritize and plan next steps

Presenter	Topic	Time
Herman	Welcome	5 minutes
Marilyn	Research Update	10 minutes
Edward & Clyde	Graphic Design Update	15 minutes
Yolanda	SEO Update	15 minutes
Elsa	Parking Lot	10 minutes
Herman	Next Steps	5 minutes

FIGURE 3.1 Meeting Agenda used by Russ Unger, (author and UX Designer based out of Chicago, Ill).

Now that you have a handy meeting template to use, you can make the promise to never send out a meeting invite without preparing an agenda and including it for the invited participants.

Workshop template

The main goal of a workshop agenda is to prepare the participants for the activity and to set the time commitment that will be required from the participants. It's best to try and keep a workshop's agenda to a single sheet. Additional pages can be added for participants to use as notepaper. If you do this, be sure to collect the notes afterward (**Figure 3.2**).

Client: [[Client Name]]
Project: [[Project Name]]
Date: Month NN, 20NN
Phase: [[Phase (eg kickoff, working session, review, etc)]]

Attendees

[[Client Name]]	[[Consultancy Name]]
Name, Role	Name, Role
Name, Role	Name, Role
Name, Role	Name, Role

Agenda

Introduction	(5)
Summary	(5)
Objectives	(5)
Workshop	([Duration of workshop time])
Next Steps	(5)

Project Summary

·   List of steps to date
·
·

Workshop Objectives

·   Objectives from workshop
·

FIGURE 3.2 Workshop Agenda used by David Farkas, a UX Designer based out of Philadelphia, Pa.

The level of depth and detail a workshop agenda needs to cover depends on the participants' level of comfort with being part of a workshop. If it's something new to an organization or team, additional content and context may be required.

Study template

Some of the more in-depth templates out there are those used to guide research activities or studies. These templates require several kinds of information that help the facilitator ensure that each session is as consistent as possible and give participants the structure needed to navigate the process.

The following study template was provided by Carol Righi User Experience Consulting (carolrighi.com). This format can be used for a variety of UX research activities, ranging from interviews to usability studies.

Depending on the environment and the setup needed to perform each study session, many things need to be done before, during, and afterward. These steps ensure that each study starts smoothly and reduces the chances that any technical issues may come up (**Figure 3.3**).

PRE-SESSION CHECKLIST
- ☐ Prepare logger.
- ☐ Prepare participant printout of participant information.
- ☐ Photocopy Model Release form and receipt.
- ☐ Prepare one-page "phony account" information.
- ☐ Clear cookies and history for the website.

POST-SESSION:
- ☐ Debrief with observers.
- ☐ Copy backup logger recording to laptop.
- ☐ Copy a backup copy of session notes to laptop.

FIGURE 3.3 Prep Checklist.

It's important to have a brief glimpse of who your participants are before meeting them for the first time. It's also a security check that lets you confirm that the participant is the same person who completed a screener if one was used in the recruitment process (**Figure 3.4**).

PARTICIPANTS							
Participant	Gender	Age	How many hours a week do you spend on the Internet?	What type of activities do you do on the Internet? Email, social networking, research, or shopping?	Comfort level with the Internet	How many times a year do you order on website.com?	Online recruits only: How often do you use www.website.com?
Melissa	F	40s	n/a	n/a	n/a	5x/month	Couple x/mo
Susan	F	40s	20hrs	All	Very	15-20	5-6x
Adrian	M	30s	40hrs	Email, social networking, product research, client interaction	Very	6	6
Jen	F	30s	20hrs	email, travel, event planning, shopping	Very	Weekly	For half of orders
Shelly	F	30s	30hrs	All	Very	20	Monthly
Les	M	60s	14hrs	Email, research, shopping, news, browsing	Very	10-12x/year	For all orders

FIGURE 3.4 Participant Snapshot.

The table for counterbalancing helps to avoid any order effect that can occur with the tasks during a study. Depending on the tasks list for a particular study, participants can learn things about future tasks while they accomplish their current task. Mixing up the task order helps to remove, or mitigate this, over all the participants involved in the study. It also helps you prepare any material that might need to be in place for the various tasks or research areas (**Figure 3.5**).

TASK COUNTERBALANCING	
Participant	Task Order
P1	1, 2, 3, 4a, 5, 6, 7, 8
P2	1, 2, 3, 4a, 6, 5, 8, 7
P3	1, 2, 3, 4a, 5, 6, 8, 7
P4	1, 2, 3, 4b, 6, 5, 7, 8
P5	1, 2, 3, 4b, 5, 6, 8, 7
P6	1, 2, 3, 4b, 6, 5, 7, 8

FIGURE 3.5 Counterbalancing.

When conducting any form of research, it's important that each study is as consistent as possible. This gives the data collected enough rigor that researcher bias can be reduced, if not eliminated. Going through an introduction script also helps you review any necessary paperwork or disclosures that may need to be signed before formally starting the session (**Figure 3.6**).

SESSION INTRODUCTION

Thank you for agreeing to take part in our usability study.

Today you'll be using [website] website to perform a few tasks. This is the way we learn about how you would normally use the website as if you were using it in your everyday life.

Now, we want to hear what you're thinking as you work, so please think out loud. Please tell us what you are doing, why you're doing it, what you are looking for, what you don't like or find confusing, what you do like, etc. It may seem a little awkward at first, but please try to talk as continuously as possible so we can learn from you as you work.

I'll be taking notes as well, so please bear with my typing. As we discussed earlier, we'll be recording this session for our internal use on the project. There will also be other people observing the session as well. But please don't be concerned—everything you do and say in this session is confidential and won't be used outside of this study.

Also, and this is very important—please remember, we are not testing you—rather, you are helping us to evaluate this website. There are no right or wrong answers. You won't be hurting my feelings if you say something negative. I didn't design what you're going be looking at today. We just want your honest feedback.

FIGURE 3.6 Introduction Script.

Just like when you speak to a large group of people, having a warm-up interview helps to put participants at ease. This can have a particularly positive effect on participants if they're in an unfamiliar environment such as a lab or conference room session (**Figure 3.7**).

INTERVIEW: SHOE WEBSITE REQUIREMENTS (5 MINUTES)

Before we start working with the website, I'd like to start with a few questions about your experiences with ordering shoes online.

    o   When you look for shoes, what are the most important factors to you? [   ]

    o   What role does price play in choosing shoes for you? [   ]

    o   Do you always use the same website to buy shoes, or do you use different ones? [   ]

    o   Do you prefer purchasing shoes via a website, by phone, or in person? Why? [   ]

    o   Think about times you've ordered something via a website (not just shoes—think of any type of website where you can place orders or purchase something). Has anything ever frustrated you to the point of leaving the website and not placing your order? What was it? [   ]

FIGURE 3.7 Opening Interview.

The task, or research area, section gives the participant the context needed to collect the valuable data you're after. This section also gives you clues to areas of discussion that may require additional probing, and reminds you of the issues you're looking to explore or observe in detail (**Figure 3.8**).

TASK 1: FIND THE WEBSITE (5 MINUTES)

This task explores how the participant finds the website—do they use a search engine, type in a URL, start at website.com, or go right to website.com.

Setup: Start at Facebook.

Happy Path:

Google Search for Company

OR

Types in website.com

Now, I'd like you to imagine that you are going to a wedding, and you need a new pair of shoes. You decide to visit [company's website] to see what they have to offer. Let's pretend you've been using Facebook. Go ahead and visit the [company's website]. [   ]

Issues to Observe:
- ○ Which search engine does the participant use, if applicable?
- ○ What does the participant type into the search field?
- ○ Which link does the participant click in the search results, if using a search engine?

FIGURE 3.8 Tasks or Research Areas.

A final note on agendas

An agenda is the first thing you create once you've completed the initial planning and preparation. It is a document that communicates the overall structure, flow, and needs of a session and conveys what will be expected from the participants. Experienced facilitators use agendas to their advantage, for agendas allow them to maintain a sense of control over the conversation and put them in a position of authority. Both of these things are necessary to run a successful session.

Chapter 4

Preparing for Personalities

I'm kind of a big deal around here...
— Ron Burgundy

One of the great wonders of the human race is that every person is unique. This wonder can wreak havoc for you as a facilitator, no matter your skill level. Past dealings with a variety of people help you prepare for certain types of personalities and behavior traits. However, it's still a crapshoot when you sit down and start the conversation about how participants will actually react during a session.

When gathering a diverse group of participants, keep this old saying in mind: "It takes all kinds to make the world go around." Likewise, it takes all kinds of people and personalities to understand complex problems and create game-changing solutions.

Creating a happy place

Regardless of the kinds of personalities in a group of participants, the best tactic is to create an environment where people feel safe to share, collaborate, and, most importantly, fail. By paying attention to participants' behavior, their reactions to one another, and their body language, you can create an atmosphere of encouragement. If participants are willing to take risks and share ideas or information that is unexpected, participants of any personality type can become productive and engaged.

Unpredictably human

Participants' unpredictability is one reason why facilitation is needed in the first place. If everyone behaved the same way, getting to the right solution for any given problem would be so easy there would be no need to facilitate anything. Getting to the proper solution takes time, collaborative conversations, and your guidance through the muddy waters of participants' mix of personalities.

Expecting the unexpected

While it's common to be surprised by what a participant says or does, it's important to never *act* surprised. This is something you should not only expect, but also encourage, depending on the nature of the behavior. If a participant unexpectedly jumps up and starts showcasing a previously unknown tool, it's an opportunity for you to discover something new and potentially groundbreaking about the subject.

It's good to have a plan for dealing with surprises because it reduces the chances of being shocked or taken off guard. If either of these occurs, the overall flow of the conversation is disturbed and it can be difficult to get the participant to begin contributing to the session again. The best tactic to take if something offensive, distracting, or otherwise attention grabbing happens is to avoid giving energy to it. Like a child screaming for attention, the more energy and attention bad behavior gets, the worse effect it has on the overall session.

Unpredictability is a good thing

Divergent behavior patterns and personalities are part of what makes facilitating rewarding in the end. When you encounter these areas of chaos, you have an opportunity to bring order to the session. Participants who are overly loud, conversational, or energetic can be used to draw out those who are quiet or timid.

Unique personalities can also help turn a session that would normally be boring or discouraging into one where all participants are engaged and provide their own content. Participants who bring energy and passion to the session not only help to inspire others, but also quickly become your best friends. These participants benefit the other members of the group and help you remain focused, passionate, and energetic. Think of naturally charismatic participants as star players in a session.

Reading body language

Gauging a participant's level of interest, excitement, temperament, and attitude can be determined by watching how someone holds himself or herself. Our bodies reveal many pieces of information about what's going on internally. If you take in the signals and react with the proper nonverbal and verbal cues, you can help bring in a participant who has checked out from the session or regulate one who is overeager. Any signal that you pick up should not be taken on its own, but rather in the full context of other body language cues to properly understand what the participant is saying.

Common stances

People naturally take certain positions when they get excited, agitated, or anxious. These stances are instinctual and go unnoticed when we reposition ourselves unconsciously to react to our surroundings. It's important to know a few of the key stances that people might take during a session. This listing isn't all-encompassing, and in some cases a particular stance may not mean what you think it does. For example, a participant might be seated with arms crossed and the chin tucked into the chest. Overall, this is a very closed stance; however, if the temperature in the room is hovering around 65 degrees it could be that the participant just happens to be cold. However, the following stances are useful guidelines if you keep alert for cues that identify the exceptions.

Hands on hips

Participants with their hands on their hips are ready for action, and that action can be positive or negative. This position is one we learn in childhood as a means to assert ourselves. It's a way to begin to show our independence. By the time we reach adulthood, placing our hands on our hips shows that we're ready to do something and we increase our personal space to ensure that no one tries to get in our way. When it's time to throw the control of the session back to the participants, look for those who are in this position. Their energy and passion can be infectious for the other members of the group.

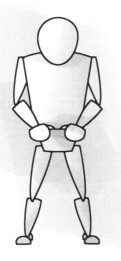

Thumbs tucked into pants

Sometimes known as the "cowboy stance," this position comes into play when one participant is sizing up another, or even you. By nature, it puts a participant into an aggressive position. This could be good or bad, depending on the other signals the participant is giving off. A participant whose thumbs are tucked in could mean that they're about to pounce on another participant, and you need to be prepared to protect the other participant or defuse the situation.

Hands on head

In some sessions, participants are required to sit at a conference table or around a room and they're able to stand up only when they "have the floor." A participant who leans back and with both hands on the back of the head is one who's ready to get up and take the floor. The participant is showing you a level of confidence and readiness that you need to be ready to react to and either support or suppress depending on the participant. This participant is ready to take a turn, and simply waiting for the current speaker to wrap up so they can easily stand up and take over.

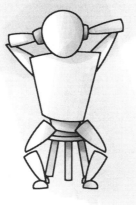

Leaning forward while sitting

Participants can easily get excited and passionate during a session. Someone who is seated when this happens will quickly get on the edge of the seat. This tells you that the participant is done sitting and being a bystander. That person is ready to jump in and add some excitement to the conversation and contribute to the session. This level of energy can be used as a catalyst to get other participants engaged and excited.

The number of body stances a participant can take are numerous, and some tell more of a story than others. Having a mental catalog of stances and their meanings can help you direct the flow and energy of a session to a greater degree.

Positive and negative arms

The motion and position of a person's arms provides a lot of insight into their mental and emotional state. The arms communicate if a person is feeling threatened, agreeable, or open to suggestion. One of the most important positions of arms is if they are positioned in a closed or open fashion. For instance, whether his arms are crossed across the chest versus relaxed and down at his sides.

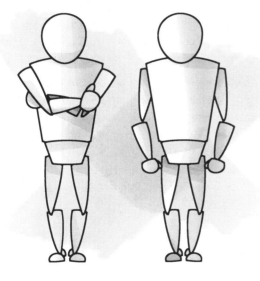

A closed position is the body's attempt to protect itself from danger. This danger could be physical or emotional, and the participant is trying to defend either himself or his ideas. Changing to open arms suggest that a participant is becoming more agreeable to the idea being presented. If a participant does enter into a closed position, there are several tricks that get them to open up again and engage in the conversation rather than remaining removed from it.

The power of a nod

The meaning of a head nod is as impactful as it is diverse. Head nods can range from the slow and steady to fast and erratic. Participants who are mulling over an idea will often slowly nod their heads as they think through the details. When the level of excitement in a session gets high and participants are in agreement with what another participant is saying, their heads quickly bounce up and down.

You can use a head nod yourself to draw out additional detail from a participant. By nodding your head at a participant as the participant shares an experience or thought, you encourage the participant to keep going. This really becomes helpful when someone does not easily share information. In situations like this, you need every trick in the book to draw information out of reluctant participant. To learn more about body language, check out Allan and Barbara Pease's book *The Definitive Book of Body Language* (Bantam, 2006) or Janine Driver's *You Say More Than You Think* (Three Rivers Press, 2011).

One technique is to get participants to do something with their hands. This could be sketching out an idea on a piece of paper, writing down notes on a diagram on the whiteboard, or looking something up on a computer. The earlier you can break the closed position, the quicker the participants become active contributors again.

Occasionally, participants will use an object to protect themselves rather than their arms. Grabbing a clipboard, coffee cup, notepad, or even a laptop is an effort to place a barrier between the participant and the topic, idea, or suggestion that is felt to be attacking them. It's important that you notice when these barriers get put up. Removing the barrier can be easy, if caught early and if participants are given something to do that allows them to voice their disagreement or discomfort in a productive way. One technique would be to suggest that they get up and contribute to a shared working space like a whiteboard.

Putting baby in the corner!

Participants are not always positive, cooperative, or engaging. Occasionally, a participant has his own agenda or reacts negatively to other participants, and turns a good session into a bad one. Part of your job is to manage a participant who has gone over to the dark side in a way that brings him back into the fold but doesn't detract from the session. There are three useful methods for dealing with a participant who begins to behave negatively. It's key to address a disruptive participant as promptly as possible, because that person's actions will quickly spoil the rest of the session.

Encourage self-regulation

The best way to deal with a disruptive participant is to let the group respond. It's best if the participants provide encouragement or suggestions to address the issue. You can foster this by encouraging participants to address issues as they arise. Here is an example:

> **John:** Well, that suggestion will never work! There is no point in us even discussing this anymore!
>
> **Facilitator:** Joan, why do you think John thinks this wouldn't work? What's he seeing that would make your idea not possible?

Directing the issue back to a different group member forces the confrontation out into the open and allows all the participants to reach a resolution. It also avoids making you the bad guy who has to reprimand one of the participants.

Taking a break

Conversations can get heated when sensitive topics come up. Participants will have strong feelings and ideas about how they would address the topic and come to a solution. These strong feelings and ideas can easily turn a healthy debate into a bickering session. Before the session reaches a tipping point and turns into a fight, it's a good idea to call a break and allow people to walk away from the conversation for a bit.

While the group is split up, you can have a private chat with participants who are proving to be overly negative or disruptive. Again, an example:

> **Facilitator:** Joe, what's going on? I can see you care a lot about this issue. What can I do to bring this conversation to some type of resolution between you and Janice?
>
> **Joe:** She just doesn't understand the direction I've been given by my directors. What she's asking for would make it appear as if we're taking a step back rather than a step forward.
>
> **Facilitator:** That makes sense. When we get back together, let's talk about that specifically and see if Janice can rethink her idea to address that concern.

Getting Joe away from the conversation was key to understanding what he is feeling and where his negative behavior was coming from. Knowing that it was making him look bad in front of his bosses helps you bring Joe back in, and progresses the conversation.

Ejection!

Eventually, a participant who continues to behave negatively and is disruptive to the other participants will cause the session to be a wash. If this happens, that makes the whole thing a waste of time, money, and manpower. You have to ensure that this doesn't happen, and sometimes that means you have to ask a participant to leave. This is not fun, comfortable, or enjoyable. This can kill a certain amount of energy and flow in the session and it's really hard to get it back.

However, there comes a point where getting the disruptive participant out of the room is more important than losing a bit of energy. The best time to ask a participant to leave is during a break. This gives that person a safe out (avoiding the embarrassment of being asked to leave) and it avoids you having to be the bad guy in front of the rest of the participants.

> **Facilitator:** Hey, Andy, it's obvious you don't want to be here and you don't see what we're doing as valuable. Why don't you let us wrap this up and I'll send you the final notes and decisions that we reach. We can talk about it tomorrow maybe?
>
> **Andy:** That works. I've got a deadline I need to be working on anyway.

The fact that Andy had a deadline might have been something that caused his disruptive behavior. He wasn't seeing value in the session, and viewed it as a distraction from something he felt he needed to be doing. Having this side conversation gave Andy "permission" to return to work and removed his negative effects from the other participants.

Preparing for patterns

Handling a diverse group of participants can be planned for, and you can make it part of your process no matter the type of session you have to manage. Even though each person's personality is unique, they generally fall into one or more personality patterns. There are many patterns out there, but it's important to have a handle on a few common ones that have a negative influence on a session when they show up.

Mr. Personality

This person has so much charisma it just oozes out of him. People naturally gravitate toward people like this and tend to follow their lead.

Imagine having Bill Clinton, known for his extreme charisma and attention-grabbing personality, in a session. Keeping and maintaining the focus of all the participants is going to be impossible. Not only that, but any participant who would like to get a little attention is going up against a juggernaut and the valuable information she wants to share will never be heard. The best approach to take with Mr. Personality is to turn him into an asset rather than a distraction. Funnel the facilitation cues and motions through him, such as getting him to kick-start a group activity rather than doing it yourself. This removes his participation from the over-all session, but capitalizes on his charisma and charm so the rest of the participants remain focused and engaged.

Teacher's pet

All she wants to do is help. Yet sometimes, her help is the last thing you need.

Every facilitator needs a helper, and it's a blessing when that helper is one of the participants. Sometimes though, having a helper can be the most unhelpful thing imaginable. A participant who eagerly attempts to help you rather than engage in the session might be feeling out of place. She may not be comfortable with what is being asked of her, and avoids the activity by trying to assist with it.

Occasionally, the helping participant can have an ulterior motive. In her head, she may think she could be a better facilitator than you are, and she may want to take control of the session. In essence, she is being a usurper. No matter what her intentions may be, you need to direct the helper back to the task at hand and retain control of your session. If reinforcing her in her role as a participant by pulling her aside during a break does not work, then as a last resort you may need to remove her from a session.

Chatterbox

He keeps going on and on and on and on. You hope he will eventually get to his point, but it becomes pretty obvious that it's not going to happen.

In most sessions, having participants talk is a good thing. It's a sign of a successful facilitator when the ideas being shared lead other participants to contribute their thoughts. Unfortunately, this environment is the perfect camouflage for the Chatterbox. A Chatterbox is a participant who gives the appearance of contributing to the conversation without actually ever saying anything of value. This behavior stems from wanting to feel knowledgeable about a subject or not wanting to be left out by the group.

You can easily turn a Chatterbox into a normal—value-creating—participant by challenging the participant to explain what he means. If ignorance is the source of the ramblings, the group will likely pick up on it and bring him up to speed. The group doesn't want to leave anyone behind, so they will self-regulate and make sure that doesn't happen.

The quiet one

This participant sits in the back and tries her best not to be noticed. She has something to say, but just assumes someone else will say it for her.

Some participants have a hard time speaking up in a crowd. This is normal, especially for people who could be classified as introverts. An introvert ends up telling an observant facilitator a lot, though nonverbally. These nonverbal cues are opportunities to engage her and to allow her to share her comments, suggestions, and ideas with the group. It's vital for you not to forget, or unintentionally ignore, a quiet participant. You'll find that introverts typically have some of the most insightful things to say. If they are ignored, they may not speak well of you when feedback is collected after the session. Try directing questions to a quiet participant, or asking her to answer or respond to another participant's last comment. If done in a very friendly and approachable manner, these are great tactics to get her to break out of her shell a bit and become more engaged in the session.

Bone picker

This is someone who shows up to push an agenda or tear down other people's ideas. He'll disagree with every suggestion or comment that gets shared, but never provide any alternatives or suggestions of his own.

Not every person who shows up to a session is there to be a positive contributor. From time to time, a participant will show up with an agenda to simply pick a bone about the topic being discussed. There are two courses of action you can take with an intentionally disruptive participant. The most productive method is to encourage the group to self-regulate the negative participant. This can be accomplished by directing the negative comments and ideas back to the other participants to challenge or discredit. At times, getting the other participants to do this can be a challenge, especially if the negative participant is of high rank or influential in the company culture.

The only option left to you, if self-regulation doesn't work, is to kindly ask the negative participant to leave the session.

The boss

Everyone has a boss, and this person is the *boss, or holds a higher rank than the other participants. She can make people nervous, and less willing to share.*

The Boss, especially one who's high ranking and carries a lot of influence or simply thinks they do, is one of the hardest personality types to deal with in a facilitated session. One of the major risks with The Boss being present in the room is that any progress or boundary-pushing ideas can get killed by a single comment. Participants who are used to having authority over the other people in the room can have a hard time letting go and letting ideas flow and gestate. The Boss also may be privy to information that makes a new concept or suggestion impossible to implement. If she shares that with the group, the flow and energy of the group is disturbed.

Handling The Boss is best done before a session starts. Ask your sponsor or host if any of the participants are authorities in the organization. Take the time to meet beforehand and explain the ground rules and the purpose of the session. During this conversation, it may become clear that The Boss's presence in the room would be counterproductive, and she will excuse herself from the activity. It's important to schedule an immediate follow-up to go over the initial results of the session and collect her feedback privately.

The danger zone

Sessions can become chaotic and negative pretty quickly, and normally it's due to one of the above personality patterns. Once a session has been thoroughly disturbed and participants stop contributing to the overall goal, it's very difficult to get it back on track and to get all the participants engaged again. Luckily, there is a period of time—the danger zone—when troublemakers have just begun to cause problems and there's still an opportunity to intervene. When a session appears to be entering the danger zone, call a break if it makes sense. While participants are grabbing a fresh cup of coffee, hitting the bathrooms, or just chitchatting with one another, pull the participant causing the issues aside and have a frank conversation with her. You must think of the group over the individual, so turning problematic participants back into productive ones takes high priority.

Finding your star players

Star players don't always naturally arise during a facilitated session. Occasionally, you have to draw them out, or help draw them out of their shells. Finding a star player is easy once you understand where participants' passions are. This can be discovered prior to the session or during it. If you don't know the participants, project sponsors, or hosts, your host should be able to provide you with a general understanding of which participants care about what topics prior to a session. During a session, pay attention to how participants react to certain topics and areas of conversation to see how you can capitalize on their personal areas of interest.

Knowing where the pressure points are allows you to quickly find these star players by lobbing questions or directing responses to a participant who is showing passion about the current topic. This takes a lot of the pressure off you and allows the participants to generate and maintain their own flow and energy.

Chapter 5

Managing the Environment

Man is a tool-using animal. Without tools
he is nothing, with tools he is all.

— Thomas Carlyle

Facilitation typically requires two things: people and words. The overhead is minimal in terms of equipment and supplies. In most cases, anything beyond people and words is typically used as additional support for the content being discussed and is not central to the discussion. Slides, for example, can help convey a point, or share content, but what's being discussed is far more important and can, or at least should be able to, happen without those slides.

Technology has made it increasingly easy to augment your sessions with laptops that can provide engaging slides, audio, video, and interactive content—and often this requires additional equipment, such as projectors, televisions, monitors, microphones, soundboards, and a remote control. You may find yourself depending on more traditional office and art supplies, such as sticky notes, markers, pens, pencils, and paper.

The more extras you add to the mix, the more responsibility you add to your own load, so be wise in choosing tools, equipment, and materials to augment your sessions.

There are two specific types of tools that you'll use: those that you provide and those that are provided for you. Using each type requires slightly different approaches and attention.

All the stuff that's yours

The tools that you own or bring to a session are fully your responsibility. That means that you must make sure they're where they should be when you need them, and that they're functioning properly. And, of course, that you need a backup plan for when things inevitably go wrong.

Your computer, software, and files need to be ready, tested, and available. Make sure you have all the files you need, including all fonts and anything else related to the information you want to share with your audience. If you plan sessions that require the use of a computer, you should also assume the cost and responsibility of having backups of all necessary content.

Meet the Expert: Richard Dalton

Richard Dalton is an Assistant Vice President, User Experience Design at USAA, and an active member of the UX community. You can follow him on Twitter at @mauvyrusset.

•

It **is** possible to adjust things like gamma and white balance on a PC, but the way you do it is dependent on the video card and its software—not the operating system—so there's no "standard" way. NVIDIA video cards are fairly common, and if you search Google images for "nvidia gamma" you'll see some screenshots of their interface.

Having said that, I've never done that when giving presentations (I've done it when trying to calibrate fixed monitors I've been using on an ongoing basis). I find that choosing fairly projector-safe colors is more effective than relying on being able to adjust a laptop/projector color combo.

Windows 7 has a display calibration tool that is buried in the Control Panel and isn't accessible from the same place that other common display settings are (**Figure 5.1**). You can learn more about how to calibrate your Windows settings here: http://windows.microsoft.com/is-IS/windows7/Calibrate-your-display.

FIGURE 5.1 NVIDIA Control Panel.

The more common adjustment with PCs is resolution: making sure you're matching the projector's native resolution so you don't get nasty scaling issues. Also, many PC laptops these days only have HDMI ports, not VGA ones, which can be a shock if you turn up and find a VGI-only projector (I made sure I got a laptop with both HDMI and VGI).

Cloud backup services are offered by dropbox.com, box.net, Amazon cloud services, and others, but remember that these require access to the Internet to access to your online content! Alternatively, you can purchase physical backup storage such as USB thumb drives and external hard drives. It's also not a bad idea to seek out extended warranty and repair services, especially if you travel with your equipment. Check with the host of your session to ensure that a backup option is available to you. As a last resort, also have a PDF of any presentation as a final backup; this will not require you to install any fonts, nor be subject to most compatibility issues, as the Adobe Acrobat Reader is a free download and preinstalled on many popular computer configurations. Projectors share what's on your computer screen to a larger screen that can be seen by your audience, which means that as long as you have a PDF, it will still make it to the screen, even if you don't have presentation software such as Keynote or PowerPoint.

In addition, you need to understand how to make your computer work with any number of projectors, televisions, monitors, or anything else that it can connect to. Not only will you need to make the physical connection from the computer to the output device, you will also need to know how to fine-tune your computer's settings so the display works properly. This means you should be aware of how to calibrate the output for certain devices, and make sure you know how to adjust the brightness, contrast, and other settings of your computer so any materials you display will be as true to your intention as possible.

Figure 5.2 shows Apple's Calibration Tool, which lets you adjust the device output settings. This is particularly useful for projected content that may require additional brightness support. Make sure you're familiar with the specific settings and controls for your computer.

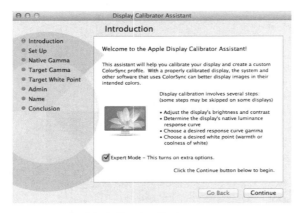

FIGURE 5.2 Apple's Calibration Tool.

Cables and connections to other devices, such as projectors and power sources, are absolutely your responsibility. If you're going to connect any of your equipment to another device for any purpose, you need to have all the crazy variants of those connections with you. If you have any questions about what those may be, speak to your host or the location where you'll be holding your session and find out what's on hand.

Make sure you have a remote control that lets you control the slides on your computer if you're using a presentation and are away from the computer during your session. Many remotes are infrared and require "line of sight" to control the computer, and those can frequently be blocked by the edge of a podium or other objects in the vicinity. The Logitech Professional Presenter R800 is a great presenting remote that has its own USB receiver and works well in most sizes of rooms. Depending on your budget, this, or a similar remote, may work well for you. Also make sure you have a spare set of backup batteries.

Plan your audio needs in advance. If you'll be playing music or other audio during your session, make sure you have the proper connections to any sound system being used, or the equipment (speakers, spare microphone, and so on) to provide an output that will properly amplify your audio and can be heard clearly in the size of the room that you'll be in.

If you provide your own microphone or headset, make sure you know everything about how it operates. Understand how to connect your microphone to an existing soundboard or PA system, as well as how to make it function optimally in the majority of scenarios.

Dan Roam, author of *Blah Blah Blah: What to Do When Words Don't Work* (Portfolio, 2011) and *The Back of the Napkin: Solving Problems and Selling Ideas with Pictures* (Portfolio, 2009), uses his own Countryman E6 Omni Omnidirectional Earset Microphone when he's speaking to a larger crowd. Roam purchased two adapters "that will match 99.9 percent of all the wireless bodypacks you'll run across," so he's prepared for just about any setting where he needs to use his microphone.

If your microphone requires batteries or a charging source, make sure these are fully charged and have backup batteries ready. Make certain that any cables and connectors required for your microphone are available and functioning, and be prepared with backups for these, as well.

Be sure that any needed office supplies are available. When office supplies are critical to your session, make sure that they're in the same place you are. If they can travel with you, take them along and make sure to keep track of them. If they're too bulky, or there are too many of them, you may want to ship them ahead of time. Steve Krug, author of *Don't Make Me Think* (New Riders, 2005), purchases and ships supplies directly to the location of his workshops and seminars through online retailers. This approach to making sure your supplies are available may require that you make arrangements with a host so materials can be delivered and inventoried prior to your arrival. If all else fails, make sure there are ample backup resources near your location so you can find the supplies that you need.

If you need the Internet for your session, make sure the Internet is where you are. This can be challenging; many sessions may require that you and your attendee(s) have Internet access . If you have not ensured that this is available, you may want to provide your own. Some mobile phone providers may allow you to use a phone as a tethering device for multiple devices, and you may want to consider the option of owning your own Wi-Fi hotspot for those instances.

Your reference materials need to be at your fingertips. Ensure that anything you plan to use as a point of reference in your sessions is with you at all times. If you travel, strongly consider putting them in your carry-on or shipping them in advance with guaranteed delivery date and time, along with a signature for traceability. In addition, consider placing any digital materials on a backup storage device or a cloud-based backup service.

Food and snacks are always appreciated. If you'll be holding a session that's more than a couple of hours long, your attendees will appreciate some food. Ensure that any catered arrangements have been made and that all information about how to enter the location and find you are in place. In addition, if you want to entice your attendees to arrive on time, food and snacks can go a long way, especially for morning and lunchtime meetings.

All the stuff that's theirs

If you're holding a session in a location you don't own or have control over, there are a number of factors you need to be aware of. Much like all the stuff that's yours, the stuff that's theirs needs to be where it should be, needs to function properly, and needs to work as it should.

And, of course, you should have a backup plan in place when any of the stuff that's theirs becomes stuff that doesn't go according to plan.

Know thy room. Do your best to learn all you can about the space you'll be working in. If you can, ask for photos, dimensions, seating arrangements, equipment location, information about outlets, and anything else you can think of that may help familiarize you with the location. Arrive early enough to give yourself time to walk the room, set up, test your equipment, and become comfortable in the space. Find out if you have environmental controls for the room, or if you're able to contact someone who is, so your attendees are less focused on room temperature and more focused on you and your topic. All of this counts as part of your planning and will help you be more at ease.

Do *not* use anyone else's computer! But, if you have to, get familiar as quickly as you can. Are there any special tips or tricks you need to know about the house (or borrowed) computer? Will it have the fonts you need? Are all the keys on the keyboard? Do any of the keys stick? Do you need to jiggle the handle to get the water to stop running? Find out so you don't disrupt the flow of your session later.

Their cables, connections, and clicker will not exist, or even worse, not work. Okay, that's a little strong, but there's a high likelihood that they'll go missing, or that the last person who used them also used them to get the gum off the bottom of her shoes. Use unknown equipment only as a last resort, and make sure you test yours prior to using it so you know you'll be at your best.

Know the extent of your audio and sound quality. Give every microphone a healthy "Testing, 1, 2, 3..." to make sure it's working correctly and that it can be heard from all locations where people may sit. If you're amplifying computer-based sounds, test those from their various sources (inside a presentation, directly from an audio or video file, and so on) in the same fashion so you get the desired outcome when you're live.

Projectors, televisions, and monitors can have limitations you never knew existed. Or, at least, limitations that you never would have thought to prepare for. If you're using a projector, ask for the specifications, including model number if you can get it, so you can search for details online. Find out how recently the bulb has been changed, what resolution sizes it can handle, where it's positioned, and where the screens are located so you can limit the amount of time you spend futzing with it and getting directly to your session. It doesn't hurt to ask if your exact make and model of computer have been connected to it before and if there have been any issues you should be aware of.

The microphone can be your friend or your enemy. Find out what kind of microphones will be provided, such as stationary podium microphones, handheld wired and wireless microphones, audience microphones, lapel or lavalier microphones, headset microphones, and so on. If you're unfamiliar with all the different types, you really need to have a discussion with your host to understand what is provided and what you, or they, are responsible for. Some establishments require that union labor perform any audio or video work for them. You'll need to know if you are responsible for operating the equipment or someone else is, and you'll need to ask some basic questions like whether there are batteries for the wireless microphones and where the power and mute buttons are, especially if you plan to use the restroom without removing a wireless microphone.

Meet the Expert: Nathan Shedroff

Nathan Shedroff, Program Chair, MBA in Design Strategy, California College of the Arts and coauthor of *Make It So: Interaction Design Lessons from Science Fiction* (Rosenfeld Media, 2012), shares some advice for dealing with displays.

•

Adjust the color settings on your Macintosh (they're in Preferences, under Display) to calibrate your display. Otherwise, you have no baseline for either seeing what you're working with or how it might appear once connected to projectors or other devices. It's also easy. Enable Expert Mode and adjust the Apple logo in each square until it basically disappears (the instructions are right there in the panel). Squint while you do all the adjustments, especially if you show video. When I present about our book, *Make It So,* we show a lot of science fiction clips and sci-fi tends to be dark. If I haven't had a chance to adjust to the projector's output (not my screen), some of the video is just a black or gray rectangle (almost no detail is visible).

Adjust the dynamic range of your photos! This makes them look brighter and better in every way. In Photoshop (if you use that), use the Levels panel and adjust each end of the histogram (graph) to the full black and white range, as well as moving the middle until the photo looks fresh and neither washed-out or dark. You can often save gray, faded, or washed-out old or new photos this way, too. If you're in iPhoto, click the Edit button and under Adjust, you have a lot of controls. The histogram at the top has the levels controls directly underneath—just like Photoshop. There are other adjustments there, too. Play with all of them but don't get too weird. Your goal is to make your photos pop but not look fake.

If you need the Internet, have enough Internet for everyone in the room. Find out how many people can be on the Internet at once, and what the password is if one is required. Test it with any Internet-connecting equipment or devices you may have. Perform speed tests so you know what you're up against. If there are network security protocols in place, make sure you have all the details to share with your attendees, and verify them yourself as soon as you can.

And always, always have a backup plan if the Internet is not available. No Internet, no cloud services! It is also a good idea to invest in thumb drives or external hard drives that are large enough to support your needs.

No tools, no problem

Clearly, there are plenty of things that can go wrong when you depend on more than words in a session. Use tools to augment good material, not replace it.

Meet the Expert: Nathan Shedroff

Nathan Shedroff, Program Chair, MBA in Design Strategy, California College of the Arts. (www.nathan.com)

•

Know your story and be prepared to tell it no matter what happens with the technology. Once, in Oslo, I was giving the keynote to a conference first thing in the morning. I got there early (always get there early if it's a foreign country—they'll tell you they have everything they need, but they often don't). It took an hour for them to find everything and I connected, adjusted, got everything set and then, right before the conference started, the other speakers came in to test their machines (thanks a lot).

I set my laptop aside on a table and about ten minutes later, one of the speakers walked by and his foot snagged the cord (this was before the MagSafe plugs) and my computer went down—right to the floor. He apologized profusely, but that computer never turned on again after that. They bumped me to the late morning and shuffled me off in a cab to the Mac repair shop in Oslo. It didn't help.

When I got back to the conference, all I had was a chalkboard—not even a whiteboard. I had to give my talk without anything I prepared *except* the story I knew I wanted to tell—and it went well. It helped that the entire audience knew what happened to my computer (sympathy often counts), but the truth is that I wasn't confined to my slides and I was much more conversational. This is a great lesson to learn—without losing your computer to learn it.

The best advice here is to make sure that whatever you need to say or hear can be said or heard using only yourself and the people who need to listen to or speak to you. Anything else, be it visual or physical (handouts, workbooks, guides, or what have you), is ideally a value-add to the experience.

Chapter 6

Practicing

If you're any good at all, you know you can be better.
—Lindsay Buckingham

I believe that we learn by practice. Whether it means to learn to dance by practicing dancing or to learn to live by practicing living, the principles are the same.
—Martha Graham

There are many opinions about the right, or best way, to practice for time as a facilitator. Facilitation happens in so many different activities that we take part in—from business meetings to telephone calls to getting up on stage and addressing an audience. The truth is, most people stumble through practicing for facilitation until they identify a way that works best for them.

We could wax poetic or provide you with a how-to guide for practicing, but instead we reached out to some of the brightest minds and best facilitators we know and asked them to share their approaches. Some of them may share techniques similar to those you may already employ, and others may offer great ideas that never really occurred to you before as you work through your preparation and practice.

Lots and lots of practice

Some of our favorite facilitators and presenters have shared their processes with us to pass along to you. He's your chance to learn from some of the best and brightest out there today.

Enjoy!

Eric L. Reiss

CEO, The FatDUX Group

A seasoned presenter and the author of several books, Eric Reiss heads a leading user-experience design company headquartered in Copenhagen, Denmark.

A great presentation helps folks think about something in a new way. There should be at least one key idea that sticks in people's brains after the presentation is over. If you can dramatize this idea in some way, the chances of it sticking are much better.

Along the way, make sure to listen to your audience. Give them an opportunity to respond to what you say, and pay particular attention to nonverbal responses, such as laughter or gasps. Ask questions, if necessary, to draw them out. If you're inflexible in your delivery, you will invariably fail.

It's basically a question of seduction. There are three steps. First, you show that you're open, friendly, and adventurous. Second, you create rapport by sharing insider information in a relaxed manner. Third, you show that you're a worthy partner by demonstrating your authority.

When I prepare for a presentation, I start by thinking a lot about why *I* was asked to present something. What is it that makes me special? And what can I give this particular audience? Only then do I start to build an outline of the presentation itself.

As to practicing, curiously, if a talk is 45 minutes or an hour, I don't need as much practice as I do for one that's 20 minutes or shorter. That's because the longer talk gives me more flexibility in my storytelling. Basically, if a talk is very short, I need to practice it *a lot*—until I almost have it down word for word.

Cennydd Bowles

Designer

Cennydd Bowles is a product designer at Twitter and the author of Undercover User Experience Design.

I try to practice a talk five times. The first run-through is usually two days in advance. (Nope, I didn't manage to write this one ahead of time either.) This rehearsal is usually a lost cause, full of embarrassed pauses and scribbled self-flagellation: "Add more detail!", "Slide 14 makes no sense," and so on.

The next one is better, and for the last couple of run-throughs I just try to thin down my notes to simple trigger words. This means I can retain some spontaneity without compromising the structure I've worked hard on.

Somehow in my rehearsals I never get the racing heartbeat and dry mouth. I've learned to add an extra minute to account for water breaks and chill-out pauses.

Nathan Shedroff

Program Chair, MBA in Design Strategy,
California College of the Arts

Nathan Shedroff is the chair of the groundbreaking MBA in Design Strategy at California College of the Arts in San Francisco.

One thing I don't do is rehearse ad nauseam. Contrary to what TED tries to counsel speakers, too much rehearsing can create a flat presentation (or one that seems like every other). Often, I practice in my head and, if it's a presentation I give somewhat regularly, I'll pull it up and run through it even when I'm not scheduled to give it anytime soon. To me, my presentation is like a conversation I have with an audience, so it's a conversation I have with myself from time to time (instead of a monologue I practice). In essence, I'm listening and speaking at the same time and, when I do this, I hear inconsistencies, hyperbole, or contradictions in what I say (as if someone else is delivering the talk). Then, I react like I would to someone else—often, skeptically, and uncover arguments or aspects I need to clarify or change.

Workshops are more difficult since they involve work from the audience or participants, not merely action from myself. I can't really rehearse or practice how others work. However, I take notes while in a workshop and make changes afterward, iterating for the next one.

Russ Unger

Co-author, Designing the Conversation

Russ is a user experience designer and researcher in the Chicago area.

Once I've identified the topic for a presentation, I find myself a nice, quiet time of day and hunker down in my office for some focused thinking and planning. Usually, this is around midnight.

When I know my topic, I know the key areas of learning that will be useful to other people, so I get out a pencil and start putting those ideas to paper. I write down as many of them as I can, adding any notes or hints as to what the deeper dive into my content is going to be. I keep going at this until I feel I've exhausted my depth on the topic.

Next, I take a look at all the content and notes that I've brain-dumped and analyze them for logical groupings. Are there multiple elements that could fit into a single category or topic area? Are there elements that overlap with various higher-level topics and could those start to emerge as a theme for the presentation? My sheet of paper ends up with a lot of hash marks, circles, arrows, and extra notes that probably make sense only to me at this point.

After tearing off that sheet of paper, I put the content together on a new sheet in the topics or categories that started to materialize on the previous page. I "box them up" and separate them into sections so I can make sure that each high-level topic area has enough content to merit its existence, and start to add and subtract content as it makes sense. Once I go through this activity, I give each section a number that indicates the flow from topic to topic. At this point I try to find a friend who will actually listen and provide harsh feedback on the idea and the flow. Ten minutes on Skype or a phone call can make all the difference in the world.

Once I feel comfortable with my content areas and flow, I fire up my favorite word processing program and write an honest-to-goodness outline based on the pencil and paper effort I've done so far. The content generally starts to really form in my mind at this point, and it gets even easier to find the gaps or disconnected parts of the presentation. This outline solidifies all the thinking I've done so far, and really feels more like I'm playing the role of my own editor.

This might seem like a good time to open up my favorite presentation software and get to work, but time has shown me that by moving my outline to large-sized note-cards using a permanent marker I can start to build my presentation as "notecard wireframes" (see, they're not dead!). By taking the notecard approach, I can start to identify my master slides and the overall design system for the presentation. I also continue to move topic areas around and tinker with structure by simply moving cards around on the wall or the floor, which helps to further work out the kinks in the material (**Figure 6.1**).

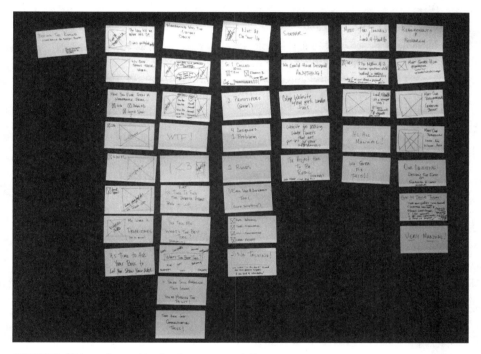

FIGURE 6.1 Notecards used to structure a presentation.

Once I'm comfortable with my notecards, I fire up Keynote and start to build out my presentation, usually laboring over font and color selection far longer than any sane person should, and then I really build out my slides in earnest.

Andy Budd

CEO, Clearleft

Andy Budd is the cofounder of Clearleft and Fontdeck. He curates the dConstruct and UX London conferences and was the inspiration behind Silverback.

To be honest we don't tend to practice for pitches, workshops, and so forth. We'll obviously plan what we'll be doing in advance, but you can never really be sure what direction they'll go in. So we tend to have a framework ready, but within that stay flexible. As such, I see it more like an improvisation than a scripted play.

However, I do practice my talks. I'll typically start practicing as soon as I've got the basic framework ready. So I'll stand in my bedroom and talk through each slide out loud to see how it sounds and check that it's making sense and the narrative is coming through. At this point I may reorganize my slides to make the talk flow better.

I like to write my talks out almost word for word. I then read through the notes half a dozen times until I've memorized the rough flow and feel confident that I know the core messages I want to get across on each slide. As such, I'm memorizing the key themes rather than a full-on script.

Once I'm happy with the slides, I do a couple dry runs on my own to get the timing and pacing right, and help consign things to memory. If possible, I'll try to get a live run-through in beforehand as well. This will often be over lunch to the rest of the team, although occasionally I may try to book in a smaller local event so I can try new material on a real audience.

It usually takes me two or three live presentations before I'm feeling completely happy with the material and have the flow and delivery down perfect.

Shay Howe

Instructor and Lead Designer, The Starter League

Shay Howe specializes in user-interface design and development. He helps co-organize Refresh Chicago, UX Happy Hour, and ChicagoCamps.

When preparing a new talk I find something I'm interested in, but perhaps a bit outside my comfort zone. I'm always trying to push myself and continuing to learn. Once I've settled on a topic, I outline the talk and briefly run it by a few people, after which I write and prepare the talk. When I'm ready, I find a group of friends, some of whom I feel to be the target audience for my talk and some of whom are experts in the field of my talk. I give them the talk and collect any constructive feedback. Taking their advice, I rework points of the talk as necessary, then get the group back together for a second run, again collecting feedback. The process provides practical experience in giving the talk while also collecting valuable feedback.

Leading up to the talk I do my best to stay prepared and alert. I want to walk in comfortable with what I'm presenting and ready to field any questions or situations that may arise. I don't eat anything crazy for a few days leading up to the talk. I avoid coffee, get a good night's rest, and try to do a bit of exercise before the talk. These are fairly common practices, but important ones. Additionally, I run through my slides an hour or two before giving the talk. The goal is to jog my brain one last time.

I always try to get into the room I'm speaking in before the presenter before me is finished, as I want the most time possible to set up. The first thing I set up is the projector, as the biggest issues can arise here. Once I'm ready, I take a deep breath and then talk to some of those in the audience to hopefully lighten the tone and get comfortable with whom I'm presenting to.

Aaron Irizarry

Experience Design Lead, HP

Aaron Irizarry is an experience design lead at HP, where he tries to improve the conversation around design on a daily basis. He also speaks on the topic of critique and design studio.

When I've put together a presentation (for work or a conference), I practice it in my home office daily (even if it feels redundant) so I get so familiar with the content, tone, and timing so that it becomes second nature.

After I feel like I have a solid grasp on the presentation, I reach out to peers to see if they're willing to be a captive audience (buying them a beer never hurts). If I'm practicing for a conference, I try to find a local meetup where I can test run the content, then I use any feedback to make adjustments as needed.

David Farkas

Lead Interaction Designer

David Farkas is a Philadelphia-based interaction designer who works on a variety of business systems and consumer goods.

Growing up, I always loved movies. And for a while I thought I wanted to go into film. I studied and read about screenplays and started understanding how to write a script of my own. So it's no surprise that when I draft a presentation, I stage my outline. After listing who my audience is and getting an understanding of the space I'll be in, I take notes on my outline of who to look at when to get my key point across. I rehearse aloud as early as possible because this isn't a report, it's a conversation. And I decide what to do with my hands (and am very thankful for a remote or notecards to keep them occupied).

Steve Baty

Principal, Meld Studios

Steve Baty is a founder and principal of Meld Studios, president of the Interaction Design Association (IxDA), founder of the UX Book Club, and co-chair of the UX Australia conference series.

My presentation style generally centers on telling a series of stories, with each having its own point and visual materials. I really don't like rehearsing, per se, and you'll never see me write a verbatim speech to deliver.

However, I do like to feel comfortable with my material, so I tend to tell other people—individuals, people at work—one of the stories from the presentation. They'll make the mistake of asking me what I'll be talking about and I launch into one of those stories.

I'm usually fairly well organized in advance of a presentation, so I can start telling those stories a few weeks ahead. By the time the date rolls around, I've told each story a half dozen times at least, and am feeling pretty comfortable with the length, the really salient points, and how to end each of them so that the next one flows smoothly.

Nishant Kothary

Founder, MINKY

After a decade split between Amazon and Microsoft, Nishant Kothary founded MINKY with his wife, two cats, and a boisterous Weimaraner.

There's ample scientific evidence that people learn best from stories. For this reason, whether it's a five-minute talk or a half-day workshop, I structure most of my presentations as stories that embrace the dramatic arc as proposed over a century ago by Gustav Freytag. It's worth noting that this doesn't work for all types of content, for example, a talk about how to build an application using Rails, but you'd be surprised at the kinds of content that are served really well by the Freytag structure.

It's difficult to talk about practicing how to tell a story without talking about the process involved in preparing it. The two are intertwined, at least as I understand it. I subscribe to the philosophy of putting in an hour of preparation—this includes research, slide design, demos, rehearsal, and so on— for every minute of my presentation. In other words, an hour-long presentation generally gets 60 hours of preparation. While this may seem like going a bit overboard, it really isn't. Consider that it's a week and a half of work for an audience of 300 (fairly typical for the talks I give) that puts in 300 hours of collective attention span.

I generally start out by creating a mind map for the story: a mental Pinterest board, if you will, of all the interesting anecdotes, evidence, demonstrations, books, articles, and so forth. Once I'm happy with that, I go through a rigorously iterative process of ordering, culling, writing the script, adding slides, and rehearsing. There's really no order. It's pure iteration with the goal of making every second as interesting as possible. The process is best characterized by Michelangelo's words, "I saw the angel in the marble and carved until I set him free." When it feels done, I present it to my wife.

Unsurprisingly, the moral to being a good presenter is: marry up.

Margot Bloomstein

Brand and Content Strategist and Principal,
Appropriate, Inc.

Margot Bloomstein is the principal of Appropriate, Inc. and author of Content Strategy at Work.

For me, preparation is less about practicing and more about priming. In every encounter, I stand on years of experience with tough clients and incisive critiques. That's the thing: There's no need to be intimidated by a podium or a pricey pitch, because you never really go in cold. In every experience, you can draw on the variety of clients, industries, personalities, budgets, cultures, and tough questions you've gathered in your past. It's that experience that likely gives you the right to be there in the first place. For me, I draw on more than a decade of ornery clients and audiences in more than a dozen industries. When I take the stage, it is evidence of the fact that I survived those experiences—and took something from them.

That sensibility lets me focus on the specific needs of the performance. Before a pitch, presentation, or big talk at a conference, I like to "prime" myself with the data, statistics, and details I need to have top of mind. Whether I'm sharing work with a potential client or a case study with an eager audience, I enjoy storytelling. That format gives color to theory and offers concrete details that humanize the topic and draw me closer to the audience.

I don't focus on practicing what I'll say because I worry that rehearsed phrases will sound canned or formal. I also don't waste time memorizing ever-changing statistics that someone could learn just as easily from Wikipedia. Instead, I prime my notes with the details. I often take the stage with a single sheet of paper on which I've marked phonetic pronunciations of tough terminology, key dates, and long names. It's simple, in the big scrawl of a Sharpie. If I'm citing a study, I note the journal in which it was published and when. If I'm sharing the results of a campaign, I jot down the company's year-over-year growth. I want hard numbers, not just superlatives. That's what my audience wants too, because that's the stuff that makes for great tweets and compelling stories back in their own companies.

Armed with those details and enthusiasm to engage my audience, I'm ready to tell them good stories, with all the facts and figures that help them come to life.

Tim Frick

Principal, Mightybytes, Inc.

Tim Frick is president of Mightybytes, Inc. (http://mightybytes.com), a creative firm in Chicago that works primarily with cause-driven clients and socially responsible businesses.

If I had to break my practice down into Twitter-sized sound bites it would be:

- Ideas discussed with coworkers over craft beers and sketched on cocktail napkins, or body parts in the absence of napkins.

- Lots of online research the next day to make sure it wasn't just the beer talking.

- More discussions with coworkers and industry friends whose opinions I trust to define the efficacy of said idea.

- Translate napkin ideas to rough Google Doc outline of learning objectives.

- Try to correlate some sort of story with bullets in outline.

- More craft beer, more ideas, more napkins.

- Magically transform Google Doc into Keynote.

- Apply rough designs to notes and research in Keynote.

- Revise design and content to the point of a rough run-through-ready slide deck.

- Rough run-through with coworkers.

- Run crying into bathroom. Look into mirror and ask, "Why do I exist?"

- Emerge smiling from bathroom and head triumphantly to nearby craft beer bar (thankfully, there are many of those in my hood).

- More revisions, more run-throughs of factual content and learning objectives.

- Revise story components, especially if humor is involved.

- Fact-check to make sure I'm not plagiarizing anyone or lying.

- Add requisite layer of icing with sparkly unicorns, rainbows, and puppies (as you know, I'm terrible at this step).

- Try like hell to get a good night's sleep.

- Sleep 2.5 hours.

- Caffeinate.

- Deep breath!

- Present.

Fred Beecher

User Experience Designer

Fred Beecher is a user experience designer at the Nerdery. Having been in this game since 1998, he now focuses on making more UX designers through apprenticeship.

When I give professional presentations, I rehearse obsessively. I memorize my intro and my conclusion because from a cognitive psychology perspective those are the two most important parts of a message. The middle I might rehearse a few times just to make sure everything flows together well and to check that I'm on or under time. But I spend most of my time with my intro and my closing. With the intro, I want to make sure I catch people's interest. I want them to know why they should spend the next 45 minutes of their lives with me. At the end I want to make sure that what I told them sinks in, so I restate my key points before going into Q&A.

Laura Creekmore

President, Creek Content

Laura Creekmore is president of Creek Content, a content strategy and information architecture consultancy focusing on health care, higher education, and other complex fields.

When I'm creating a presentation, I do a lot of consolidation work. For instance, I start with a big outline, and then I rearrange things as I do the real creation. I wouldn't call it "writing" as much as creation—I'm thinking about how concepts fit together and thinking about the visuals and the pacing as much or more as I'm wordsmithing.

Even before I've finished the presentation draft, I talk out parts of it out loud, which always leads to my changing things significantly from my initial outline. As I'm creating, then, I'm editing all along the way.

Then I give the presentation many times. Occasionally I practice in front of other people, but I really get a lot out of a mirror, too. I also travel with a projector when I'm speaking out of town so I can practice in my hotel room.

No matter what I'm doing in front of an audience, I find that it helps a lot to think about what I want the audience to take away from the experience. I try to think of myself as a vehicle for a message, and then focus on the most effective way to deliver the message. It gets me out of my head a little bit so I don't worry as much about whether Laura Creekmore is embarrassed in front of groups—I'm just a conduit.

Bill DeRouchey

Principal Designer, GE

Bill DeRouchey is a principal designer in the design and experience group at GE, where he turns battleships, step by step.

Every now and then, I'll give a public presentation. Maybe 20 minutes, maybe 45, but invariably I end up on a stage, a tiny mic clipped to my shirt, pretending to sound smart about design or technology in front of hundreds of people. And even though I still get nervous beforehand every single time, I now know to expect it, accept it—and just power through it.

My presentations tend to have a linear story, a build from beginning to end. So I better know that story. Luckily, or by design, because I've been working on this presentation for a while, I know the subject well enough to be able to riff on it and talk a bit off the cuff. That can be dangerous. On stage in front of hundreds is not the place I feel comfortable just making stuff up.

So I practice. Since I usually speak at conferences, I'm living in a hotel a day or three prior to my presentation, away from my happy, comfortable home. I practice my presentation two or three times before speaking. I stand up in my room—standing feels more real, sitting feels more constricted. I start a timer so I have a sense of whether I'm going over or under my allotted time. I hold my presenter mouse in hand to advance slides. And then I talk. I force myself to talk slower. And pause. Because a presentation cadence is a bit different from conversation cadence.

Invariably when I practice out loud, I say lines I've never thought before. If a line is good, I stop the timer, write it in the presenter notes, and then resume timing and talking. If a transition feels clunky or out of place, I stop, shuffle, and restart. I just keep going to the end. If I have time, I do it again immediately. I also try to practice at least once a few hours before I go on live so everything is fresh.

One more thing about sleep: Normally you'd think that getting a solid night's sleep would be the smartest thing to do, and it probably is. But I've noticed a pattern in myself where if I don't get much sleep the night before, because of time zones or going out with fellow conference attendees, my speech has a nice mellow cadence to it. I'm tired, and because I'm tired, I'm slower in a good way. My speech is measured, and frankly, I'm too zonked to have the pre-speaking jitters. It can't be a smart practice, but it's nevertheless interesting.

Nick Disabato

Interaction Designer

Nick Disabato is a freelance interaction designer and publisher from Chicago.

I find it really challenging to memorize talks to the point where I'm comfortable with giving them, and I get nervous with any content that's sufficiently complex and unfamiliar to me. So, I rehearse a new talk ten times before I give it.

I write the whole thing out in presenter notes, and those serve as the training wheels that I need to get familiar with my talk's structure and content. As my own free time goes, I've found it challenging to repeatedly break out an unbroken, hour-long block of time to practice a presentation. And the first few times I run through it, I always want to make a bunch of edits to the notes, because something doesn't flow right or I want to clarify an important point. It's hard to resist that in the middle of a run-through.

Dale Sande

Another UI Guy

Dale Sande is a maker of things, a general do-gooder, and a vanquisher of evil. He loves the HTMLs, the CSSs (really Sass), the JavaScripts, the Rubies, and the Rails.

Call it reckless, but I rarely practice for any presentation I give. Interestingly enough, the very reason I got into presenting with groups and now conferences was not to simply present, but to engage. I guess you could say I'm more of a performance artist, if you will.

There are topics that I'm very passionate about, and I've found the best way to engage others was to give presentations. This is not to say that I don't try to give a solid presentation and I don't do ample research; in fact, it's the opposite. I work hard to be prepared for any topic that may arise during my presentation.

To me, giving a presentation and looking to assemble workshops as well is not a dictation. Presenters who simply stand there and read from a script are uninteresting and flat to me, regardless how awesome their subject is.

I guess, in the end, my presentations are my practice sessions. From each experience I take away what went well and what fell flat. Oddly enough, I've found the more I rehearse and prepare what I'm going to say, the less interesting the outcome is. The more I come to know the material, have supporting visuals, and just run with the conversation, the more successful I am.

Ross Belmont

Chief Experience Designer

Ross Belmont gave up a life of code to build the design practice at Appiphony, a Chicago-based consultancy focused on Salesforce.com apps.

Before we pitch a design concept to a client, I pitch it internally to the engagement manager and engineers on the project. In addition to being a round of practice, it forces me to nail down the user's flow through the scenario to tell a coherent story. The engineers analyze the concept's technical feasibility and almost always throw in one or two good design suggestions. Even better, the joint decision-making ensures that we'll walk into the client pitch with a unified front.

How should you practice?

Now that you've reviewed the approaches to practicing from these talented professionals, your job is simple: learn from them. Read their stories and pull out the pieces that make the most sense to you. Follow some of them exactly if it fits into your own personal style, or make your practicing mash-up based on the examples here. Or find your own way and create a personal approach that works for you.

Section 2

Group Facilitation

The facilitation of groups occasionally feels more like herding cats than guiding people through a defined process. It's important to know the various types of group facilitation that you may be called upon to perform and the special considerations for those activities. This lets you start with your best foot forward, and end with the valuable content you were asked to produce with the group.

Chapter 7

Workshops

Individually, we are one drop.
Together, we are an ocean.

— Ryunosuke Satoro

Two heads are better than one, right? Why is this not true for ten or twenty heads? It turns out it can be, when they're guided by a skilled and effective facilitator. Workshops take a lot of time not only to plan, but also to prepare for, including the work that must be done on the day of the workshop itself. This time is necessary to ensure that the workshop goes off without a hitch and that the participants produce quality content and contribute as best they can.

Taxonomy of workshops

There are many different types of workshops you can find yourself facilitating during your career. The specific type of workshop you end up running will differ based on audience size, intent, and environment. Typically though, workshops will fall into one of three categories: kickoff, exploratory, and decision making.

Kickoffs

Kickoffs are unique because they not only set the tone for a project, but also educate the participants about the rules of engagement for the project. Every project has a set of rules that are intended to lead the project team to success, and it is during the kickoff workshop that these rules are detailed and described. These rules inform project team members about how they are to behave with other team members and what roles will be defined for the project team, and lays out at a high level each team member's expected accomplishments. Kickoff workshops actually happen twice for any given project: first for your team and compatriots and finally with the project's sponsors and stakeholders.

Meet the Expert: Kevin Hoffman

Kevin Hoffman is an information architect and design strategist who has been building stuff with bits and pixels since 1995. He leads digital strategy projects for a wide variety of well-known brands in higher education, gaming, museums, type foundries, radio and television, power companies, and more. He appreciates your valuable time; he'll thank you personally if you contact him at kevinmhoffman.com.

Regardless of whether you're starting a project with your internal team or the full project team, the purpose of a kickoff is to get the ball rolling. The activities contained within a kickoff help to progress all the work that will need to occur over the course of the project. You're not going to create the final work products during this time, but getting them started helps to get all the parties present engaged. An important aspect of any kickoff is the cataloging and description of the activities to come. These activities could be occurring over the next few days, or the next few months. Getting people exposed to the process and the effort that will be required is essential to establishing a positive project culture.

With a project culture successfully in place, the overall awareness of the project increases. The stakeholders who are directly involved will have a better understanding of the problem and how that problem needs to be resolved. People within the organization who hear about the project around their respective water coolers may become interested enough that they inject themselves into the process and provide unexpected value. These hidden sources of information can help make the project a success, because they've either attempted to solve the problem themselves in the past or may be aware of issues that would have put the project at major risk.

Internal kickoffs

Hosting a kickoff with the assigned project team, prior to the official project kick-off, is a good way to debrief the team on the history of the project and determine what everyone's role is going to be during the project. Not giving the working team members this opportunity to learn the context of the project poses a great risk, because people will be playing catch-up from day one. It's best to take the time to get everyone in the same room, or on the phone, and express your understanding of the project and what it will take to be successful. This includes an overview of roles, responsibilities, and timelines.

For any kickoff to be successful, it needs to be attended by people from as many different departments and disciplines as possible. Each person involved brings a different point of view, unique ideas about how the problem should be fixed, and experiences working within a specific area of an organization that other participants might be missing. All these different perspectives give you plenty of material to use during the workshops or in later workshops.

To arm yourself with the necessary information and context around your new project, take the time prior to the kickoff workshop to do on-the-ground research. This is the time to do stakeholder interviews to learn about the organization's business, culture, and language. After the interviews, add what you've learned to your own past experiences and expertise so you come to the kickoff workshops more informed and prepared. You'll be able to speak to the problems that plague the organizations, and in many cases, point out the real problem that the project needs to solve—not the one that was listed in the project brief or state of work.

All this upfront research, stakeholder involvement, and cross-department involvement builds trust between you and the project sponsors. It is folly to think that just because you won that work that you have the trust of the client out of the gate. Don't confuse getting hired to do the job with being trusted to get the job done. This is where good facilitation skills become really important. Being a good facilitator ensures that every participant in the workshop is treated equal and it distributes the problem and possible solutions across the whole group. Successfully facilitating a kickoff workshop, or any type of workshop, also shows that the money it cost to put on the workshop was worth it. Workshops are not cheap, because every participant involved earns a salary and in many cases that salary is substantial.

Good facilitation skills may not exactly help you build trust, but these skills will help you maintain the trust you've built with the overall project team over the life of the relationship or project.

Some team members may not be aware of the overall timeline of the project or the official kickoff workshop with the external partners. When covering the timeline, pay close attention to the planned activities. Allow the other team members to weigh in on what they think of the activities and bring up any that may be missing from the plan. As Kevin Hoffman states:

> **Make the internal kickoff a design meeting for planning the big meetings that are to come. Allow the team to discuss all the things that need to occur during the project and begin to trim activities that simply do not make sense.**

The kickoff.

External kickoffs

Kickoffs with a client or separate department and team happen for every project. These workshops tell the project team and stakeholders "Work has begun on Project X!" It's an important event, and one that deserves the care and attention to get it right. Project kickoffs unofficially begin once the time has been set for the workshop and people agree to be present. Once this has occurred, it's time to start planning and preparing for what people will be learning versus doing during the formal kickoff.

Exploratory workshops

Exploratory workshops focus on exploring the knowledge of the participants and encouraging participants to explore a problem area, situation, or topic area. These types of workshops give you, the project team, and general participants insight into the domain knowledge that stakeholders take for granted. Not every solution has to be the same old wheel; occasionally, people have already created an ad hoc, or inappropriate, solution to a problem that you can take advantage of. Getting people in the same room, focused on an activity that they may or may not be familiar with, allows them to communicate these solutions that may have become second nature to them.

Exploratory workshops are also good for taking advantage of the creative problem-solving abilities of others. Stakeholders are intimately aware of the good and the bad attributes of the environment they have to operate in. However, they don't always know how to communicate these experiences. In this situation you might give participants a visualization exercise to force them to think about the topic on hand a bit differently. Suddenly they're sharing past experiences in a way that lets you gain a deeper understanding that can be useful later on in the project.

Decision-making workshops

Decision-making workshops bring together a group of experts or stakeholders to make a decision about an important topic. These can set the stage for a new strategy that the team or business will be following, or help the team decide if one solution is better than another. As the facilitator, you should know that when workshops are meant to *result* in a decision, participants are most likely going to show up with a decision already in mind. It is your job, over the course of the workshop, to get participants whose minds are made up to reach a general consensus and get the undecided participants to determine which option deserves their support.

As the facilitator of a decision-based workshop, you must guide these two groups through a structure and meaningful argument, or debate. When you know that participants will come to the workshop with either a decision in mind or are open to persuasion, you need to create an environment that allows each side to communicate constructively until a majority has been reached. These workshops can sometimes be a bit hairy, as participants are passionate about the direction the decision is headed in, so don't be afraid to force breaks or even throw in a distraction or two to keep heads cool and collected.

Check out *Gamestorming: A Playbook for Innovators, Rulebreakers, and Changemakers* by Dave Gray, Sunni Brown, and James Macanufo for a great collection of workshops and activities (www.gogamestorm.com).

Defining the purpose

Every workshop needs a stated purpose that informs participants why they need to attend and why their input is important. In many organizations, the idea of spending an hour or two (or longer) in a workshop is still foreign. In others, it's not foreign but it requires strong justification, because workshops can be very expensive depending on the cost per hour to conduct the workshop. A strong purpose validates both the cost of the workshop and the overall investment required to pull it off.

During the first few moments of the workshop is your chance to validate any of these concerns and get people focused on the task at hand.

Give a short history lesson

Take some time at the beginning of a workshop to provide participants with a history of what led to that particular workshop. Even if it's one in a series that has occurred over the course of a week, speak to how each workshop ties into the other and how the results of one fuel the beginning of another. An overview of past events and workshops also gives participants the chance to get settled and become familiar with all the people involved. This is really important for participants who only get involved in a single workshop and don't get the exposure to the whole series of events. It shows the depth of the work that's been done, or is yet to come, and may increase participant engagement since they know their ideas and voices are valued enough to be included.

You're invited

In theory, everyone who gets invited to a workshop should know why they were included. However, it's safer to assume that people don't always read the message tied to the invitation and require a little background as to why they are there. A quick overview explaining why each participant, or group of participants, was invited helps them focus on specific topic areas that will be covered during the workshop.

Participants want to know that the time they're devoting to the workshop will be worthwhile; this is your chance to give them that confidence. If participants feel that they really *need* to be in your workshop, they'll be less likely to let their minds wander to the pile of work on their desk or in their inbox.

Shooting for the goal

During the introduction of the workshop, you'll need to properly describe the outcome the workshop will produce. This gives the participants involved the focus they need to get started and helps to bring forth content that will ultimately be what helps you or the project team. Remember, not every workshop results in a concrete product. When this is the case, you'll need to set the parameters for what sort of content collection you're hoping to get from the participants. This ensures that the content participants provide goes to some end goal, even if it's not visible right away.

Setting expectations

Expectations help you, as the facilitator, provide the necessary guidance to participants so they can easily start interacting with the assigned activity. A key aspect of the guidance you'll be providing is to set the expectations for the purpose of the workshop and the type of content you are there to collect. The best way to do this is by telling the participants what will be covered, what will *not* be covered, and what topics will be the focus. This helps to put all the participants on the same page and on equal footing.

Defining the boundaries

Boundaries are important for all workshops, especially those that mean to explore specific context or content space. Expressing where participants are allowed to go, and areas they should avoid, helps the workshop maintain a flow and a purpose. If you allow the participants to go off on tangents that don't relate to the goal of the workshop, not only will you fail to collect the content the workshop is meant to produce, but you'll also have wasted the participants' time. Remember, workshops can be difficult to schedule due to the availability of participants and space, and the cost per hour that goes along with conducting them. Taking the time to validate the cost of the workshop helps in scheduling future workshops.

Facilitating for flow

Workshops are like a good play: they have an opening, middle, and closing that leaves all the participants fulfilled and exhausted. Facilitating workshops is about moving participants through this flow and doing it as naturally as possible so the workshop does not come across as contrived.

Meet the Experts: Aaron Irizarry and Adam Connor

Aaron Irizarry, left, is an Experience Design Consultant for HP who shapes design process and facilitation for the web platform design teams.

Adam Connor, right, is an Experience Design Director for Mad*Pow and an independent illustrator based in western Massachusetts. As a designer, he has spent much of his career exploring collaboration, critique, and the design process, and he uses what he's learned to help organizations improve their design capabilities.

•

Why is proper critique necessary in a workshop? How does critique affect the outcome of the workshop?

Often, the goal of a workshop is to first generate and share a variety of ideas for a design, solution, and so on, and from there to build consensus toward one (or a small number) of the strongest ideas that will be pursued after the workshop. It's a common mistake to think that your position in an organization is a reflection of the validity of your ideas or observations. It's important that, if our goal is to create and build the best "thing" possible, we start from a position of everyone's thoughts being on a level playing field. Everyone is equal. By paying attention to the quality of the critique occurring in your workshop and using previously agreed-upon goals, personas, scenarios, design principles, or whatever other criteria you have for a project, you can focus discussions and work to avoid personal opinion wars, and hierarchically influenced discussions (read: directives).

How do you properly instruct workshop participants on the language of critique?

The most important thing is to first explain what critique is. It's not just a gut reaction. It's not judgment. It's a comparison of the design or idea you're evaluating against the goals and objectives the creator is trying to satisfy with it. Critique language focuses on a few key points:

- What goal was the creator trying to satisfy or what problem was he or she trying to solve?

- How did the creator try to satisfy that goal or solve that problem?

- What is the perceived effect of what the creator did? Do you think it meets the goal or solves the problem?

At the same time, this structure/language can be used to identify goals or problems that the designer has not yet attempted to solve. If there is an agreed-upon goal for the effort, and a participant in the critique asks how a design or idea satisfies the goal, and the creator cannot answer the question, then you've identified an area for improvement and iteration. The creator now knows that he or she has missed something that the project team has agreed is important, because it was already set as a goal of the project, and on the next iteration steps should be taken to address it.

What are some common rules or constraints that participants need to be aware of when providing critique?

There are four main rules that help ensure a good critique.

- **Try to avoid problem solving and design decisions.** It's almost instinctual, especially for designers, that when we identify an issue, we begin to envision a solution to it. Oftentimes, rather than describe an issue entirely (its cause, impact, and so on), people will jump straight to describing what the solution should be. We see this all the time in critiques, but it's problematic for a few reasons:

  - It moves away from the focus of the current activity. You should be focusing your attention on evaluating and understanding the design or idea you're reviewing. As you move away into describing some theoretical other solution, you've taken the focus away from that goal.

  - The human brain can't think creatively and analytically at the same time. Instead it operates more like a binary switch. As you begin describing this other solution, some people will switch their mode of thinking to trying to envision and analyze it; some will still be trying to analyze the design they're looking at; and some will likely start trying to come up with another solution. The resulting conversation will be very difficult to keep focused.

  - It can often be premature. Depending on the scope of this new idea, it may not take into account enough of the other interactions, goals, functionality, and other aspects of the entire project.

- **Everyone is equal.** As mentioned previously, it's important during a critique that you not let personal opinion wars or organizational hierarchy distract or deter from the evaluation of the design. Having an agreed-upon foundation for the product or design you're creating is critical to your ability to do this. The strongest tools we've seen for this are personas, scenarios, goals, and design principles. If the team agrees to these prior to generating ideas, they serve as a centering tool for conversations. In addition to these, there are numerous lists of best practices for various facets of design that can be referred to.

- **The creator is responsible for design decisions and follow-up.** The goal of a critique is to further the understanding of the design decisions made so far and their impact, not to modify the design itself—hence the preceding rules. Coming out of the critique, it is the creator's responsibility to use this new understanding in deciding how best to iterate on the design.

- **Everyone's a critic.** Conversational dynamic is important in critique. The best critiques are discussions. Even though many critiques may start off awkwardly, it's important to try to facilitate them toward a relaxed discussion as quickly as possible. Ignoring the role of a dedicated facilitator for a moment, having silent participants is detrimental.

sidebar continues on next page

Meet the Experts: Aaron Irizarry and Adam Connor (continued)

Participants who don't say anything can hurt a dynamic, leaving people wondering why they aren't talking, and leading to continued discomfort and awkwardness throughout the critique.

This is why, as part of facilitating a critique, it's important to note how people are participating. If people are silent, ask them directly for their feedback. It's OK to put them on the spot. You can also follow up with them one-on-one afterward. It may be that they're uncomfortable in a group setting.

Is there ever a time you don't want critique to occur in a workshop? Why?

Yes, primarily during any divergent thinking styled activity. One of the main challenges to generating lots of ideas is the tendency to toggle our brains between creative (generative) and analytical thinking. To come up with lots of ideas for a problem, it's important that we do whatever we can to keep people out of an analytical mindset.

When should the facilitator participate in the critique periods of a workshop? Why?

Much of this depends on the structure of the activity. If the facilitator is acting as a dedicated facilitator for the entire workshop, then ideally he or she would never participate in the critique. If the facilitator is acting as a contributor during the workshop as well, then he or she should contribute in the critiques of any work they've contributed to. You want participants to be able to think both generatively and analytically. If you allow them to participate one way, you should give them the opportunity to participate in the other.

Relying on your agenda

Remember the meeting outline you created in Chapter 3, "Set the Agenda"? This tool is your saving grace to maintain the flow of a workshop. Your agenda gives you the necessary structure to move from one topic to another, and sets time limits for each topic so you cover all the content you need to draw out of the participants. If there's one sheet of paper you constantly carry around with you during the facilitation of a workshop, it should be your agenda. Never let it leave your side.

Tick tock goes the clock

During the planning phases, a one- or two-hour workshop doesn't sound too long. But once you get started, it's easy for time to get away from you as participants begin to create content and you get engaged in their conversation. Before you know it, the workshop is half over and you've covered only a third of what you needed to. You have three options for keeping track of time. You can consult the clock if one is present in the room. If there's no clock, you can rely on your wristwatch. Be careful doing this though: Looking at your watch can give participants the impression that you're bored and just want the workshop to be over. Finally, a very visible way of managing the clock is to set a timer with a stopwatch or your phone. If you choose to use your phone, make it very apparent that that's what you're using your phone for because, again, it can give the impression you're simply looking for a distraction.

Freedom to diverge

Participants require some freedom to explore and think about the topic of the workshop. For workshops that aim to explore a content area or come to some sort of resolution, this freedom to explore is crucial. If you choose to give participants chances to dive deep into a topic, scheduled or otherwise, don't let it detract from the other subjects that need to be covered. Giving participants this chance to explore among themselves can help them come to a resolution sooner or bring up ideas, concepts, or experiences that may not have been discovered otherwise.

The language of critique

Many types of workshops end up producing a huge number of new ideas and concepts that can be used by the project team. Not all ideas are created equal, however. Instructing and encouraging participants to properly critique the ideas being produced prior to wrapping up is vital. This critique helps to uncover new constraints and requirements, but it also provides the project team with insight into the priority and importance of the content created by the group.

Workshop fallout

The final outcome of workshops typically takes two forms: more content than you know what to do with and excitement from the stakeholders involved in your workshop. The degree of excitement gives you some insight into how successful your workshop was, but it also helps to validate the investment that was made in the workshop. What really helps convince the senior sponsors, stakeholders, or your boss that the workshop was worth it is being able to do something with the content collected.

Wrap it up

With any facilitated session, it's crucial that you end a little early or at the very least on time. Workshops take a lot of energy out of you and the participants, and you don't want to be the person who keeps tired people trapped in a conference room. A warning sign to look out for is the energy level of the participants in general at the end of a workshop. If it's high, you may not have gotten them involved enough in the activity and really taxed their brains; you want that energy spent during the workshop so they're drained by the end. If they're dead on their feet, give yourself a pat on the back for running what is likely a successful workshop.

Closing time

As the end of a workshop approaches, walk around and start collecting the material that was generated earlier on or material the participants are done with that you will use afterward. This will be a subtle hint to participants that it is time to wrap up their own activities or conversations. Once the focus is back on you and you have everyone's attention, begin a round of questions and answers and collect some feedback on the workshop.

Question and answer time is really important because this is where you lock down the follow-up sessions that need to occur. Ask what times work best for participants so that when you start scheduling these sessions, the participants will already be expecting them.

Spend a few minutes right before you give everyone the OK to leave to collect some on-the-spot feedback on how well you did as a facilitator and how the participants felt about the workshop. A common means of doing this is a positives and deltas chart (**Table 7.1**). It's important to simply collect what others tell you and not try to defend your facilitation style or the inner workings of the workshop. Just collect the feedback and deal with it internally later.

TABLE 7.1 Positive and Deltas Chart

POSITIVES	DELTAS (THINGS TO CHANGE FOR NEXT TIME)
Really engaged everyone.	Provide a bit more instruction up front.
It was nice to see everyone's ideas posted around the room.	Give us a practice round to get used to the activity.
We thought about the problem from a different angle.	

All about the results

It's been mentioned before in the chapter, but it bears repeating: Workshops can be a very expensive, but if done correctly they are invaluable. The results of a workshop are your best friend when it comes to proving the ROI of the sessions. Take the time after your workshops to thoroughly comb through all the material and results and put it into a digestible report that you can send or present to the key project stakeholders, for example, a PowerPoint presentation that provides an overview of the activity, the names of the participants involved, and the key findings that came out of it. This recap can not only spawn additional in-depth conversation, but also document the event and the value it provided to your project and the entire organization.

Chapter 8

Brainstorming

The most creative spaces are those which hurl us together. It is the human friction that makes the sparks.
— Johah Lehrer

Back in the days when the hot air of whirring overhead projectors and the smell of warm grease pencils filled most conference rooms, deep in the heart of a generic hotel at an annual meeting of a conservative Midwestern company, a roomful of salespeople sat silently by candlelight.

At the end of a long conference table sat a man with Tibetan tingshas inches from his face. He swung his hands together and the bronze cymbals sounded, filling the room with a single, clear note.

"Picture in your mind's eye a small and delicate flower floating gently inside your skull," said Gordon MacKenzie, longtime Hallmark Cards corporate manager. After leading the group in a guided meditation session, MacKenzie turned the lights back on and, according to the account in his book *Orbiting the Giant Hairball* (Viking, 1996):

> **The group exploded. . . . People were listening, seizing others' ideas, and vaulting to the next plateau.**

MacKenzie had done what every successful brainstorming facilitator must do: he unlocked the expertise of others. He had accomplished it by allowing them to step outside the gray-suit culture of their organization. Today, shiny white, black-screened, ultrathin devices hum almost imperceptibly in most conference rooms, but we remain as constrained by the status quo as ever.

The value of brainstorming

Brainstorming is the generation and evolution of ideas by a group of diverse individuals. Ideally, it takes place in an atmosphere that feels relaxed and nonjudgmental—and a bit subversive.

Tom Willis, a real estate services executive who runs brainstorming sessions for high-end condo associations, helps people break out of the status quo: "It helps their brain get out of business as usual because half the time, we're doing these sessions because business as usual isn't going too well."

Alex Osborn, the advertising executive who in the early 1950s created brainstorming, favored quantity over quality. His concept was that if you can generate a hundred ideas, some of them will be good. The problem is there isn't actually a statistical distribution model that can guarantee that even one of them will be any damn good. It's just not the same as estimating how many cherry seeds in a bag will end up producing a tree.

Brainstorming has evolved to address problems with enough variables to confound earlier, volume-based methods. People aren't looking for a hundred cool ideas about anything; they just want the one that will work.

Facilitated effectively, the same energy squandered on "blue-sky" brainstorming can instead be directed toward addressing specific problems. Constraints can be introduced in more sophisticated brainstorming, constraints that spark innovation rather than quashing it. Brainstorming delivers tangible results, determining product direction, developing more effective processes, and collaboratively crafting strategy.

Constraints

People tend be more creative when working within constraints than when they are encouraged to create with no boundaries. But not all constraints spark creativity.

Constraints that help:

- A well-defined problem that participants must address (an iPhone app's original name gets truncated on the home screen, for example)
- Just enough context to suggest structure (goals for the brainstorm, for example)
- Base guidelines that introduce some elements of reality (the law of gravity, for example, limits aircraft design)

Constraints that hurt:

- Restrictions disguised as constraints (an iPhone app's name must conform to outdated branding guidelines, for example)
- Too much context (a complete history of the exercises that preceded the brainstorm, for example)

How to run a successful brainstorm

Unfortunately, for many organizations "let's brainstorm" is a nervous tic. Whenever they think they need innovation, they plop people in a room and expect all challenges to magically disappear an hour later. But successful brainstorming requires careful planning and skilled facilitation. Sara DeWitt, Vice President of PBS KIDS Interactive, and a serial workshopper, says:

> If you're not managing the group in the room and helping direct the brainstorming, you're going to end up with a lot of nonsense. It can't just be a crutch. You still have to put some work into it in order to generate the best possible results from the team.

Planning before the session

Facilitating a brainstorm effectively is a very specific skill that can be honed only by doing it. It is intense and demanding. However, the hardest work for brainstorming often takes place in preparation.

Problem and goal definition

To facilitate effectively, you need a solid understanding of the problem for which the brainstorming session is being conducted. Share that problem with participants if the knowledge provides useful context, or shield them from it if it hinders their creativity.

Once the problem is well defined, goals for the session can be addressed. You may need to work with stakeholders to identify the session's goals and be particularly mindful about how they are introduced to participants. Options include:

Generated goals: When participants help craft the goals for the session, they tend to be much more invested in the outcome.

Validated goals: Sometimes, others within the organization may set the session goals and preserving the participants' opportunity to improve them can increase their engagement.

Mandated goals: Some facilitators prefer to generate goals with little flexibility.

Participants

Ideally, a list of invitees is made up of just two kinds of participants: the talent and the stakeholders. The talent are those with the highest probability of delivering what the facilitator needs; the stakeholders are individuals who could disrupt the effort if not invited.

The participants might be asked to prepare as well. For a design brainstorm, they might be asked to study or review websites, mobile applications, or other interfaces. For other types of brainstorms, participants may be asked to read blogs in advance, conduct market research, or scour magazines for inspiration.

Facilitating during the session

There are no standards for brainstorming activities because the choice depends on the skills of the facilitator, the abilities of the participants, and the culture of the organization. Each activity should be planned in a way that answers the question: "What could you do with this group of people to best achieve goal X?"

Tactics

During the session, always employ and rely on these five tactics:

1. Use questions to lead conversations. Humans feel compelled to respond to just about anything delivered in the form of a question. Right?

2. Protect the timid. Brainstorming can be scary for some and rather than fighting that, the facilitator should take full responsibility for allowing participants to react in their own way to the brainstorming environment.

3. Encourage the bold. If someone risks experiencing embarrassment by participating, the facilitator needs to lavish that individual with praise and appreciation.

4. Embrace surprises. The best material often comes from unexpected sources at unforeseen moments.

5. End early. There's no better proof that the facilitator values the participants' time than giving some of it back.

Agenda

Some facilitators choose to walk participants through an agenda. This can be important when there are participants who don't yet trust the facilitator not to waste their time. Others keep the agenda to themselves so they can adjust it on the fly without disrupting the flow of the meeting to announce the revisions.

Notes

Notetaking is transformed during brainstorms from a private task to a collaborative experience. As much as possible, both text and images should be part of notetaking and every other activity because, as Dan Roam says in his book *Blah Blah Blah: What to Do When Words Don't Work,* "To solve the problems of today, we need to see and hear, read and look, write and draw."

Capturing notes in a brainstorm is more like painting a portrait than writing a book. Linear, comprehensive recording is less important than illustrating concepts as they're discussed. Those illustrations can evolve and combine with (or separate from) other related concepts as the conversation progresses.

Try to secure the largest drawing space available (if whiteboards or giant sticky notes aren't available, find butcher's paper) and make sure there are enough markers for everyone in the room. While, as facilitator, you may choose to do most of the capturing, you have the option of sharing with a notetaker or with one or many of the participants.

Notetaking in a brainstorming session should get your participants thinking visually, sharing ownership over ideas and feeling that their contributions have been heard by the group.

Communicating after the session

To optimize the value of a brainstorm, you have to accomplish one more task as participants slip back into their day-to-day skins. If you can deliver a succinct email before the end of the day that outlines the brainstorm's key successes or most important ideas, a very interesting thing will happen.

The same people who hours earlier may have fought pitched battles over any point or detail during the brainstorm will agree with your email statement of that same point. (To make the magic happen, you must describe the point with the same integrity that existed during the session.)

Keep the whole email to less than a laptop screen in length and make sure to use the simplest language possible to maximize credibility and effectiveness.

Meet the Expert: Julia Stewart

Julia Stewart is the Director of User Experience for Discovery's Education division.

•

One of the more exciting creative brainstorming experiences I've had was with Fred Rogers (the creator of Mister Rogers' Neighborhood, the children's series that ran for more than thirty years on public television.) We were tasked with creating a visualization of the 3-D animations of his trolley world. Fred told a story about how to set up a situation where kids are most creative. If you give them nothing at all to play with, they're not going to know where to start. Give them a plastic truck that has all the bells and whistles and kids will play, but they really won't be engaged. But if you give them a block that looks like a truck and disks that look like wheels and maybe with something else that looks like a horn, they'll put it together and create stories around it and participate and spend a lot of time playing with that item. They're able to infuse their own imagination with these elementary forms to create a sense of play and story.

What makes a good brainstorm facilitator?

Think about what it takes to facilitate a brainstorm: You have to lead a group of people to a place you couldn't have gotten to by yourself and that they couldn't have found without you. So while the skills involved are useful for all facilitation, the combination of those skills is somewhat unique.

Sensitivity

You should be able to read the reactions and energy in the room. People are intimidated by drawing and writing and thinking in front of others and empathy makes for better facilitators. When facilitators move around, when they speak and act with passion, when they support and endorse the work of others, it invigorates and empowers the group.

Honesty

You make a contract with each person in the room. Attendees risk embarrassment in front of their peers, direct reports, and supervisors. To earn and be worthy of that risk, you must be as honest as possible and act with great integrity. In doing so, you create a safe environment where failure isn't just tolerated, but actively encouraged as the truly productive force that it is.

Leadership

You have to capture the participants' attention and hold onto it for the duration of the session. A facilitator has to help people whose attention may otherwise have a tendency to wander. Elizabeth Eckert, a project manager for the consulting firm Sapient, has helped run a dozen intense workshops:

> You need to know when to push the boundaries and to take a certain point in another direction. The wider group is there to brainstorm and toss ideas back and forth so it can't be scripted towards a certain direction, but [the facilitator] needs to be able to understand and juggle many different pieces to find that piece that they should have gone to.

Preparation

Never begin a session before arming yourself with all the tools and knowledge you need to be successful, even if that means starting late.

A sense of humor

You won't grow a sense of humor if you don't already have one, so this can't be a requirement for good facilitation. But humor can be a powerful tool. Tom Willis says:

> Good humor always is a little bit unexpected and out of the box and isn't that what this process is about? Sometimes it gets you out of a particular pattern and into a different one. But it doesn't work for everybody. Some people just aren't that funny. And if you force it, it's horrible—and very uncomfortable.

Sneakiness

Be honest in your dealings with participants, but not necessarily transparent about all matters. Sara DeWitt, for example, isn't above rigging the audience:

> It helps to have a few people in the room already on board with what you know you want to do to kind of help with the room.

> I've also texted people in meetings if I'm sitting all the way at the other end of the table and I know they have good ideas that would help other people in the room, but are being lame about it.

What brainstorming does

Brainstorming will not cure cancer. It will not transform people who have exhibited limited creativity into amazing innovators. And it will not convert a staid, conservative organization into a cutting-edge dynamo.

But if a session's goals have been well defined, its guest list carefully crafted, and its activities intentionally and skillfully facilitated, brainstorming can generate concepts and solutions far outside the limits of the status quo.

When Gordon MacKenzie shook up Hallmark Cards' annual sales conference, he had no illusions about achieving permanent change. Brainstorming doesn't alter culture. It's a mercenary act intended only to collect the unique data that addresses a well-defined challenge before disappearing back into the night. MacKenzie writes:

> The escape from habitual culture must always be temporary if you wish to be permitted back into that culture.

> 'Yes, you may go out and play; but you must be home by dinner time.'

Chapter 9

Focus Groups

I have opinions of my own, strong opinions,
but I don't always agree with them.
— George H. W. Bush

Opinions, they say, are like assholes; everyone has one, and everyone thinks everyone else's stinks. Focus groups apparently bring a lot of stink together in a single room, with the sole purpose of gathering a bunch of opinions from carefully selected participants. It's easy to look at focus groups with disdain and call their effectiveness into question, but when used and conducted correctly, that stink can be a nice scent that makes the room pleasant to be in.

The focus group

A focus group is a qualitative research method for listening to and gathering information from a group of people. The emphasis is on the word *qualitative*; the nature of the focus group is to allow people to speak freely about specific topics, either their own thoughts or in response to the other participants in the group.

Focus groups are great for getting select groups of people to come together to discuss a topic or topics in a common language. When members of the group start to discuss and share their opinions and experiences, other members can find something that they can relate to, which results in a snowball effect with the others in the group. These are the types of discussions that other kinds of interviews may fall short of, and they are important to be aware of when choosing the focus group over another method. While some people have little problem with self-disclosure, it can be difficult for others.

The players

The core of a focus group consists of a moderator/facilitator (or lead moderator), selected participants, additional moderators/notetakers, observers, and a location.

The moderator/facilitator is responsible for not only listening to the participants, but also guiding them on the journey of getting information out into the open. The moderator can help a less-engaged and participating closed group dive deeper into a topic by listening closely for cues that can, with a little nudging, bring about more lively discussion. In addition, the moderator can steer the group toward a new topic to keep the conversation focused and on track.

Selected participants are those who've been chosen to take part in the focus group. That may seem obvious, but this group of people has been selected from a broader group of potential participants because they map to some demographic(s), area of expertise, or other trait. Focus groups are not generally composed of randomly selected individuals, although the selected group makeup may be randomized to help reduce bias.

Additional moderators, notetakers, and observers may be more than a little useful when setting up a focus group. Open discussions can yield a lot of information and can be too much for a single person to attempt to take on. While most focus groups are recorded, live notetaking can help reduce the time to generate an output or report of findings and recommendations as well. Observers, particularly those who are out of sight and observing via remote access or behind the glass, can be very useful to the process. This is especially true if those observers happen to be stakeholders, members of your project or product team, or most importantly, clients. By simply taking part in a focus group through observation, stakeholders can gain more insight immediately than any report of findings could ever hope to deliver.

As Jared Spool, founder of User Interface Engineering (http://uie.com), says:

> **The tipping point came when we found teams where all these other folks were participating in the user research studies. No longer did they assert their own opinions of the design direction above what the research findings were telling the teams. Having the execs, stakeholders, and other non-design folks part of the exposure program produced a more user-focused process overall (www.uie.com/articles/user_exposure_hours).**

The location is also quite important, but it doesn't have to be a physical location. It's most valuable to get all the members of a focus group in one place; nonverbal cues provide the moderator with an opportunity to dive deep for more information or redirect, or even understand, if a participant is not on the same page as the group. In times of restricted or reduced budgets, travel and facilities costs may make it worthwhile to consider an alternative virtual scenario such as an audio and video teleconference where all participants and the moderator can be seen and heard. While seeing and hearing the participants will always be the ideal options, there are other, less engaging options. You may want to use a chat room or a private online forum where the responses are all typed, but keep in mind that a lot of opportunity for exploration and understanding can be lost when there's little actual interaction with the participants.

Group size

Opinions as to the optimal group size will vary based on who you speak to, but based on our research, the smart size range, depending upon your type of focus group, time, budget, and type of information you are seeking, will likely be between four to eight participants for smaller groups or six to ten participants for larger groups. This may come across as an attempt to be slightly humorous, but the size range is important—you want to work with a manageable group, and you want to make sure that the time you spend with each group allows each participant enough time to provide quality feedback.

When you break this down to simple averages, a focus group with 10 people that fits into a 60-minute time slot allows you only six minutes of information from each participant. When you triple that time, you're still only getting about 18 minutes from each participant—at the very most—but you're also forcing 10 people, plus a facilitator and support staff, to give up three hours of their time.

As you consider the size of the group, think about the number of questions you hope to get answered, as well as the total number of participants, and the amount of time you've allotted. How many questions can you get answered from a single participant in six minutes? Twelve? Eighteen? Be realistic; it may make sense to add additional groups that are more intimate in order to get better information.

Number of groups

When you're planning to run focus groups, look across your segments and plan for three to four focus groups for each. This is when focus groups start to look a little hairy and hectic, but keep in mind that if each group runs between 60 and 120 minutes, you can run three to six groups in a single day. The more groups you run, the more coordinating of schedules and allocating of incentive funds you'll need to do. If, in addition to different participant segments, you also have to factor in different markets, you could end up doing a lot of focus group work.

The math works like this: If you have three user segments, and you run three focus groups for each, that's a total of nine focus groups. If you need to run these focus groups across three markets, you're now up to 27 different focus groups, which is a lot of focus groups, and a lot of time, and potentially a lot of cost for the sessions. Likewise, any reporting outputs will likely take more time as you collect more data, so be certain to set expectations accordingly for this.

As always, time and budget may constrain your ability to perform as many focus groups as you'd like to, so work the sliding scales to find your best results given the restraints you have in place.

Recruitment

It never fails: Someone, somewhere, on some project proclaims that "everyone" is their target audience/market/user, so you should be able to include everyone in your groups. The reality is that you really need to isolate the core members of your groups, and set out to recruit those types of people.

Sometimes, recruitment can happen from lists of qualified customers generated by a client or product owner. Sometimes you may place an ad online and have your potential participants fill out screeners and then run filters against your results to generate lists. Whatever the mechanism, you may need to be the person who does the actual recruiting and confirms the appointments with the participants.

When speaking to potential participants, it's important to set the stage for why you're contacting them—make sure they know that you're not selling them anything, and that you're contacting them for their assistance about the topic, product, service, or the like. Give the participants all the relevant information about the dates and times available to them, and ask them to confirm their attendance. Make them aware that you'll follow up with them and in what way (telephone, email, or other means) to remind them of their commitment.

Question planning and preparation

It's reasonable to allow for about 10 minutes of discussion among the group for each question you want to ask. The math is simple, but the questions may appear deceptively so; ask a person to tell you what they do in their day-to-day at work and you may end up spending 30 minutes on a single participant.

Focus group interviews

Chapter 11, "Interviews," describes several types of interviews and techniques for conducting them. Focus groups are a bit of a different beast in that you're attempting to get a specific number of questions answered in a finite amount of time *and* get participation from each member of the group. As you think about that for a moment, it's easy to see how you'll need to draw on all of your facilitation skills to pull this off—you can have a variety of personalities that may want to monopolize a conversation or not participate at all, and one of those types can influence the others as the conversation keeps going. You'll need to keep your group on task, on track, and on time if you hope to get all the data points that you're looking for! When you're planning and preparing for your focus groups, the following are essential to helping you:

Identify the goals of the focus group. When you're planning your questions for the group, make sure you set realistic goals for what you want to obtain from the group. That is, what is it that you want at the end of the group, from the group? Without defined goals, you can find yourself in the middle of a bunch of discussions that get you nowhere substantial.

More questions and more participants require more time. As mentioned before, it's very important to limit the amount of questions you're going to ask to fit the amount of time that's available. The formula goes like this: Amount of time divided by number of questions divided by number of participants. Here's an example: 120 minutes divided by 10 questions divided by 10 participants equals 1.2 minutes of discussion time per participant per question. That doesn't include time to kick off and wind down the focus group, so plan your groups appropriately to help you get the data points you need.

Open-ended questions get long-form answers. Well, hopefully. If you ask questions that can be answered with a simple yes or no, you're likely to get yes or no answers with limited discussion. You should strive to ask questions that allow for discussion. You should also make sure that your questions aren't leading; participants should, through their discussion, bring answers to you and not the other way around. You don't want to guide a participant to an answer that has such a tight focus that additional information cannot be, or is not easily, uncovered. Rehearse your questions with others to ensure you are not setting yourself up for limited responses that you may have inadvertently led your participants to.

Feel free to use follow-up questions to add specificity to your primary questions. Some of these you can plan for, and some you may need to formulate on an impromptu basis. When you practice your questions, some of them may be uncovered and help you in the live sessions.

As the moderator of a focus group, it's important to get insight into the questions—and hopefully you're a part of the question-generating process—so you can ensure that the questions are presented in a common language and in a way that allows the participants to feel comfortable giving an answer. The questions should be mostly open-ended, or a yes/no answer with an explanation to support the response. Keep your questions short and simple, and make sure that they're easy to understand.

Make sure that your questions have a logical flow, and consider the following as your questioning route:

- **Opening**—This question gets all the participants talking at the start of the focus group so they feel included and engaged.

- **Introductory**—This question provides the topic of discussion to the group and gets the participants focused.

- **Transition**—These questions help guide the participants along and are a logical continuation from the introductory question, as well as movement toward the key questions.

- **Key questions**—These questions are the key purpose of the focus group and are essential to the findings and reporting that you'll do after the sessions are complete.

- **Ending questions**—These questions close out the session and give participants the opportunity to think of any information that they may have forgotten to provide earlier.

For additional information on creating a questioning route, see Richard Krueger and Mary Anne Casey's book *Focus Groups: A Practical Guide for Applied Research* (Sage 2009), which provides a detailed description of these (page 41).

Hold the reins to the group. Group dynamics are difficult to predict. You may end up with very dominant personalities (see Chapter 4, "Preparing for Personalities," for additional insight) who take over the conversation. Likewise, you may end up with personalities who do not feel comfortable sharing their views with others for a variety of reasons. Part of your job as the facilitator is to direct attention away from the personalities who try to take over, as well as to steer the silent types toward the conversation.

No one said this was easy!

Incentives

When you ask someone to participate in your focus group, it's important to remember that they're committing to providing you with access to their time, in addition to potentially taking time to travel to and from your location. Time is a valuable commodity and needs to be compensated fairly.

Fair, unfortunately, is viewed differently from person to person, if not project to project and client to client. Policies for providing incentives also vary from company to company, so you'll need to understand the policies in place prior to promising any type of compensation.

As a general rule, start looking at compensation value in terms of the value of the time of the participants. Take the estimated average salary for your participant group and calculate an hourly rate. Factor in travel time and any other time necessary for their participation in the focus group. When in doubt, round up as best as you can; if you provide too little compensation you may make it easier for a participant to miss your session. Provide too much and you may find yourself on the losing end of the budget sheet before you even get started.

If you're unable to provide monetary compensation, remember that people, in general, like to share their opinions and thoughts, so they may be willing to help out with your focus group provided it doesn't cost them financially to do so. If you have an option to schedule your focus groups during nonworking hours or provide some other form of compensation (a nice meal, discounted products or services, complimentary products or services, or the like), you can still find a lot of success.

Focus groups: How will I know?

Focus groups aren't always the best method for performing research. Focus groups will not be your ideal choice if you want to perform usability testing or you are seeking statistical data. Usability testing is best performed in a one-on-one scenario, and each participant can perform tasks based on his or her normal behaviors and without the input or influence of others. Statistical data is best served from less open-ended discussions, and potentially from surveys that require specific answers.

Focus groups are best used when you want to learn how different segments or groups feel about a topic, or if you want to gain insight into how different ideas may be received by different groups of people.

The television industry frequently runs focus groups to determine how well show pilots are received prior to assigning them to a lineup. Likewise, the movie industry may run focus groups to test how an ending to a movie fares with specific groups prior to a full-scale launch. The response from the groups helps to guide decisions about what's done next.

According to Krueger and Casey, focus groups have evolved into a variety of different types, most notably market research, academic research, public/nonprofit, and participatory. Each of these groups has a slightly different purpose and approach, and knowing about them can help you understand not only what kind of focus group you should be doing, but also whether or not you should consider using a focus group at all.

- **Market research focus groups** are what most people think of when they think of focus groups. These groups tend to include about 10 to 12 participants, and are run in rooms that have one-way mirrors with people (notetakers, advertising and marketing team members, product designers and developers, and any other stakeholder interested in learning more) observing behind the glass (and likely eating M&Ms or some other finger snacks). These focus groups usually focus on consumer products and the participants' opinions about them.

- **Academic research focus groups** tend to be less formal than their market research counterparts, and may be smaller, with about five to eight participants. These focus more on issues of community, solidarity, public health, education, policy issues, and so on, and are likely to be in a more casual setting, meaning that there probably won't be a one-way mirror and hidden observers.

- **Public/nonprofit focus groups** are usually targeted to groups of about five to eight participants in a much more casual setting, such as a living room or a community center, also without the one-way mirror and hidden observers. In addition, the entire process is much more transparent and the research may be shared with the participants and the community.

- **Participatory focus groups** also have about five to eight participants and can involve research professionals mixed with non-researcher volunteers. They're typically done on tight budgets and can be challenging to pull together from a coordination perspective. There's a lot of training and coaching that needs to be done, and inexperienced researchers may stray from guidelines and scripts that have been provided to them, which can result in less rigorous outcomes in the data.

While Krueger and Casey have identified these approaches, remember that they are broader categories and styles that can be used. If you have fewer participants, it doesn't mean you're excluded from market research focus groups.

In a discussion with Chris Risdon, interaction designer at Adaptive Path, it became obvious that you could modify a focus group to review work you've put together based on other interviews and interactions with people. If you've created an experience map based on the way that certain people perform tasks in their day-to-day work, you could pull together a focus group to review the results of your previous research.

Meet the Expert: Chris Risdon

Chris Risdon is a lead experience designer at Adaptive Path. He started a journeyman career in information architecture and product strategy in 1997, and over the past 14 years has applied a combination of IA and graphic and interaction design thinking to successful products and services for both large enterprises and start-ups.

•

An experience map visually describes how a service or product system is experienced. It shows the user's journey through different touchpoints that afford or characterize a customer's interactions.

In the end, what you're striving to do is tell a story, in a visual way, using synthesized input (qualitative research, quantitative input, and so on) from customers or end-users. A focus group is a great way to get those customers directly involved in this process. Through a structured and well-facilitated focus group, you can validate the story told through the map with actual customers. It's a cognitive walkthrough, but zoomed up to the journey level instead of the task level—a chance to confirm, or modify, your conclusions from your initial research. Focus group participants can help you validate your current-state experience map, and collaboratively help build a future-state experience. Their feedback, discussing how they'd like the journey to be experienced, adds another layer of research input and can help identify where to focus and be a catalyst for moving toward that future-state.

At its simplest level, an experience map as a focus group tool provides a great visual reference around which to organize a discussion. It can become an aid in removing some of the abstraction from their own descriptions of their individual experiences, providing a shared frame of reference for the session.

In many cases, focus groups will not be the right choice. Make sure you fully understand the purpose for running a focus group, and make certain that the type of qualitative information that you're going to receive is the kind you'll need to make the right decisions.

That was easy, wasn't it?

From the perspective of a researcher or designer, user experience or otherwise, focus groups mean that there's more work to be done to map the findings to results or recommendations. This is not a bad thing, mind you, but it's something that you should consider before doing a focus group.

Meet the Expert: Josie Scott

Josephine (Josie) Scott is a user experience design researcher at GE Capital in Michigan, specializing in research, testing and facilitating aha moments—then synthesizing insight into solutions.

•

Everybody has to have some experience when running a focus group—the focus groups require that you pull from all of your other experience, be it usability testing, public speaking, running workshops, or other types of working with people. You need to be able to read nonverbal cues, body language, and to some degree, the minds of your participants.

Mentorship and coaching is ideal, if not essential, when preparing to run a focus group. If you want to run a focus group well, it should not be your first attempt at moderating or facilitating. Instead of spinning one plate, you're now spinning several and each of them is full!

Focus groups may appear simple from the outside, but there are many aspects to planning and running them successfully. You'll be flexing all of your facilitation muscles when you take them on, so your planning, preparation, and practice are essential to your success.

Chapter 10

Participatory Design

As we have seen there is some kind of continuity in any case since every experience affects for better or worse the attitudes which help decide the quality of further experiences, by setting up certain preference and aversion, and making it easier or harder to act for this or that end.

— John Dewey

The origin of participatory design is generally credited to Scandinavian initiatives in the 1970s, first in Norway, where computer professionals worked closely with ironworker and metalworker union leaders and members on the integration of new technologies in the workplace.[1] Talking, listening, and observing sometimes simply are not enough. Sometimes you need to get people engaged and involved in the design process to get the results that you're seeking.

When that is the case, there are a variety of participatory design activities at your disposal. As a facilitator, it's your job to have enough information to plan and prepare for the participatory design sessions, and the skill to keep the activity moving along.

---

1   Winograd, Terry, ed. "Participatory Design" in *Bringing Design to Software*, New York: Addison-Wesley, 1996.

What is participatory design?

Participatory design is what happens when you bring people—business stakeholders, employees, business partners, customers, people who are using the thing—into the design process. It is a blended, team-based approach to design that gets a group of people who are invested in the final outcome together—the participatory design is the process and the final outcome.

Rob Moore, customer experience design manager at Liberty Mutual Insurance, calls participatory design "the idea of placing objects within a context and allowing people to experience those objects." You're creating a condition where other people can participate in the design process, and you get to guide them through it.

Meet the Expert: James Macanufo

James Macanufo is a coauthor of *Gamestorming* and a thought leader in facilitation and interaction design. He is cofounder of Signal Workshop and former director of consulting at XPLANE, the Visual Thinking Company.

•

More and more, everything that is designed is done so in a participatory way, and this is largely a good thing. Take any product or service—a web app or a toy or a credit card—if it's a part of people's lives, they can stake a claim in how it works and what it means. By doing some participatory design you're recognizing that, and bringing people into a process where they can have an explicit voice in the shape of what you're aiming to create. This means that everyone—customers and everyone else on the team—is involved. There are no spectators allowed. If run right, a process like this can lead to happier people and better products; if not it can waste everyone's time and crash good ideas with groupthink. The stakes here task designers with learning a new skillset: not just designing amazing things, but also amazing ways in which those things get designed.

How to do it

Participatory design is not without its upfront preparation and planning. If you're attempting to redesign a home page for an organization, you'll need to understand what the needs and goals are for the home page and the organization. Then you need to determine who are the right people to have in attendance. And then, well, then you need to get some design done.

Planning and preparation

You need the right group of individuals, and you need to get them all together at the same time. Everyone in attendance should have an attachment, or an investment in the design process or the outcome. Ideally, you want a variety of people, including the users of what you're designing and the business stakeholders who are investing in and counting on the outcome.

Determine a set of discussion points that will provide your group with a unified set of information to work from. You may want to revisit questions from stakeholder interviews or create a set of new ones, but prior to beginning any design activities, a discussion can ensure that all baggage is left behind and any tensions or differences are resolved and agreed upon.

Removing friction

I (Russ) once worked on a project where the marketing person and the CEO had distinctly different goals, objectives, and ideas about what our final product was supposed to look like, as I discovered during the stakeholder interviews. I sensed that this could not only hurt the project deadlines and completion, but that I would be serving too many masters if I couldn't get this resolved. When we were going through participatory design activities, I started by bringing up the points that were most contentious between those two parties and was very fortunate—they were able to find consensus and agreed on a direction in our discussion and discovery. That kept us on track and minimized the amount of back-and-forth I had to manage, and both my client and I were happier for it.

These discussion points can be as simple as asking or reaffirming:

- What are the primary goals of the home page? Secondary goals?
- What is the priority of the goals? Which are must-haves and which are nice-to-haves?

You can also readdress any issues or concerns that were uncovered during your preliminary research or stakeholder interviews, to make sure that you give your participants a uniform set of information to work from. You may need to deep-dive into details, such as providing a clear understanding of what a registration and log-in process looks like from a technology and development perspective.

Designing

The range of activities at your disposal from a participatory design perspective can at first be overwhelming, particularly if you're setting one up for the first time. (Also review Chapter 7, "Workshops," for more information on this topic.)

One of the most common and easiest-to-perform activities involves common office supplies that you likely have at your disposal: large sticky notes, notecards, and markers.

Sample participatory design activity

Objective: Design the home page for ChicagoCamps.org

Primary goals

- Provide users with an overview of the active and upcoming camps being planned for the organization.
- Allow users to instantly register for any active camp.
- Provide users with an opportunity to get involved through sponsorship, speaking, or volunteering.

Secondary goals

- Provide users with information from social media streams.
- Share testimonials from previous camp attendees.
- Allow users to sign up for the mailing list.

Provide participants with notecards and markers, and facilitate the discussion around the goals. When the goals start to become more specific, prompt the participants to stop talking about what they look like, and start sketching them. Assure them that this is not about being in the fine arts, but instead to get ideas onto paper (**Figure 10.1**).

FIGURE 10.1 Sketch of the testimonials goal.

There can be more than one

There are many varieties of participatory design activities to choose from. The sample activity in this chapter is a lot like using Colorforms (www.colorforms.com) for websites: it lets your participants move the pieces around on the page template without making firm decisions and drives team understanding and consensus. You may choose to print a variety of user interface elements, such as those available at UXPin (http://uxpin.com) or Keynote Kung-Fu (http://keynotekungfu.com/) for different platforms (mobile phone, tablet, kiosk) and allow participants to get very specific with their design intent.

Once the sketches are complete, ask the participants to place them on a representative home page template (whiteboard, large sticky note, or the like) (**Figure 10.2**).

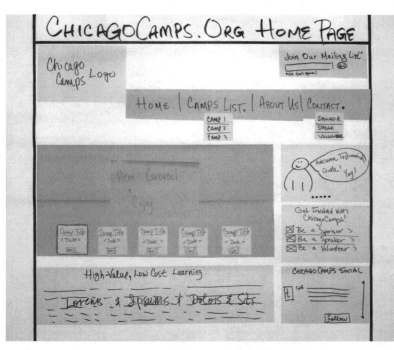

FIGURE 10.2 Home page created by the design participants.

Repeat this until all the primary and secondary goals have either found a place on the home page or have been deprioritized.

The good news is that there are some smart people who have provided you with some excellent options to choose from.

- **Gamestorming** by Dave Gray, Sunni Brown, and James Macanufo (O'Reilly Media, 2010) provides dozens of activities that can be used to gather a variety of information through play. Many of these can be used as part of your planning and preparation or information gathering, as well. You can find more activities at the Gamestorming website: http://www.gogamestorm.com.

- **Universal Methods of Design** by Bella Martin and Bruce Hanington contains a hundred different approaches to design methods, including several focused specifically on participatory design activities.

You can choose an activity, such as Design the Box, for participants who may be timid about drawing (**Figure 10.3**). Break participants into groups and provide them with a large cereal box, colored paper, scissors, markers, and glue or tape, and ask them to design the physical package for their product, service, or website. The participants start to map their goals to different "blocks" in varying sizes, and cover the box, based on their interpretation of the priorities of the goals. Once completed, the groups present and critique the ideas to one another and obtain additional feedback.

FIGURE 10.3 Design the Box activity for a grade school website's home page.

You can learn more about Design the Box at http://www.gogamestorm.com/?p=576.

In addition to the design of websites, applications, devices, and other, more tangible objects, Rob Moore has taken to using participatory design in an approach that he calls "business envisioning labs," which take into consideration the real-world context of what's being designed.

Meet the Expert: Rob Moore

Rob Moore is Customer Experience Design Manager at Liberty Mutual Insurance. He has over 25 years of design leadership experience across a variety of industries. Rob is passionate about providing a source of continuous innovation for businesses and extraordinary experiences for their customers.

•

Business envisioning labs combine elements of participatory design and scenario planning to create an immersive environment for business participants (and their partners) to engage in planning and direction-setting activities within the context of a prescribed future state for the business, its market, and value web.

A business envisioning lab can be easily reconfigured around a variety of future states to allow participants to explore various product, service, and brand scenarios in a controlled way. A business envisioning lab can evolve from a UX project team room by arranging research insights, frameworks, and concepts within the context of market and industry variables. By adjusting the context, designers can broaden the array of solutions and present all solutions within a concise set of business assumptions.

Over time, a business envisioning lab may become a more formal space that represents a particular "vision of the future" for the business—and demonstrates how its products and services will exist in that future. This type of immersive experience can demonstrate a compelling point of view for business leaders and their partners.

Participatory design awareness

As with any approach, participatory design isn't always the right answer for the problem you're facing. You may deal with people who are uncomfortable turning design over to a group, and you may need to provide them with some additional information to pull off the activity. Once you understand the challenges and benefits, you'll be able to make more informed decisions about whether or not participatory design is what you need, and if so, what types of activities you can plan.

Challenges

As a facilitator, participatory design can test the limits of your skill. You may be working with people who've never designed a thing in their life, and they may be intimidated by the entire notion of the activity. You're tasked with keeping the design activities moving, but you also need to make sure that your group doesn't overlook opportunities to go deep in unconsidered and valuable territory.

The Abilene Paradox by Dr. Jerry B. Harvey (Jossey-Bass, 1988)

The original story is from the book The Abilene Paradox and Other Meditations on Management *by Jerry B. Harvey (Jossey-Bass, 1988).*

On a hot afternoon visiting in Coleman, Texas, the family is comfortably playing dominoes on a porch, until the father-in-law suggests that they take a trip to Abilene (53 miles north) for dinner. The wife says, "Sounds like a great idea." The husband, despite having reservations because the drive is long and hot, thinks that his preferences must be out of step with the group and says, "Sounds good to me. I just hope your mother wants to go." The mother-in-law then says, "Of course I want to go. I haven't been to Abilene in a long time."

The drive *is* hot, dusty, and long. When they arrive at the cafeteria, the food is as bad as the drive. They arrive back home four hours later, exhausted.

One of them dishonestly says, "It was a great trip, wasn't it?" The mother-in-law says that, actually, she would rather have stayed home, but went along since the other three were so enthusiastic. The husband says, "I wasn't delighted to be doing what we were doing. I only went to satisfy the rest of you." The wife says, "I just went along to keep you happy. I would have had to be crazy to want to go out in the heat like that." The father-in-law then says that he only suggested it because he thought the others might be bored.

The group sits back, perplexed that they together decided to take a trip which none of them wanted. They each would have preferred to sit comfortably, but did not admit to it when they still had time to enjoy the afternoon.

Source: Wikipedia (http://en.wikipedia.org/wiki/Abilene_paradox)

You need to be able to spot if the group is falling victim to social pressures to not rock the boat or to play it safe. The group could make poor decisions by following the first option presented instead of offering resistance or alternatives. Groupthink and similar pitfalls are not the only challenges to be aware of. Sunni Brown shares some of the more common challenges she's met with in participatory design activities.

Meet the Expert: Sunni Brown

Sunni Brown is an international speaker and author who runs a visual-thinking consultancy. She is also the leader of the Doodle Revolution, a global campaign for visual literacy.

•

The arrival of people in entirely different contextual understandings. A big part of facilitating involves bringing people to a common ground from which to work. The different experience levels of the participants can be simultaneously an obstacle and a benefit. A good facilitator needs to know how to design a process that leverages the *shared* skills, awareness, and experience of the participants, but also allows specific expertise of an individual to elevate or clarify the conversation. Knowing when to keep the group together and when to distinguish a particular member of the group for their knowledge takes finesse and discernment. The goal is to move the participants toward a shared outcome, while also accommodating their unique talents and points of view. Generally speaking, the needs of the many outweigh the needs of the few, but the few still warrant attention and consideration during the design *and* the facilitation process.

The necessity of empathy operating at a 360-degree level. At times, it will be next to impossible for you to get a really clear understanding of what your participants experience in their daily work. You won't be able to know the work politics, you won't be able to know their obstacles, you won't really know the sacrifices people endure or the triumphs they feel. In these circumstances, it can be useful to present yourself as the consummate newbie. What you can then offer the group is the presence of a person who has no preconceptions of how they operate. You can be a fresh lens on what's possible for their team and an open space in which they can see themselves and their roles anew. This involves having your antennas wide open and letting the group teach you what they know. Through that empathic leadership, people suddenly have an opportunity to change.

The leadership having a specific outcome designed in advance. Sometimes, leadership can have implicit or unstated motives for group work and they may want to steer the group in a particular direction or toward a particular idea, while presenting the session as if it's genuinely open-ended and participatory. Avoid being a pawn or a puppet for leadership's intentions, because it compromises your integrity with the group and they can sniff disingenuousness even if there are only two parts per billion. Try and sift out these scenarios prior to agreeing to facilitate a session, and be very clear with yourself and with leadership about where your boundaries are.

sidebar continues on next page

> **Meet the Expert: Sunni Brown** (continued)
>
> **Knowing when to stop being rigid about the process and the time.** Agendas are designed to be broken. Go into the facilitation session with a meticulously designed agenda, knowing full well that you may need to turn on a dime. Your job is to move the group toward a credible and appropriate outcome, not to have them plow through meaningless shit just because you designed it. Be prepared to change the game, ask unplanned questions, break up the groups, stop the clock. Pull the plug when something isn't working well. Don't spend the group's time or energy on an activity if the benefit in doing so is fading fast.
>
> **Not being able to dictate the ethics of the group.** You're a facilitator, so ultimately you're in service to the group and to the leadership of the group. This means that you don't get to tell them how to act or what to believe in. There will be times when you'll see team dynamics that are painful to watch; you'll see leadership without merit; you'll see rampant delusion. You can carefully offer your perspective, but that doesn't mean you won't have to surrender it. You may be the leader of the meeting, but you're not the arbiter of their realities, so if you have any rescuing or herding tendencies, there will be times when you'll need to gracefully relinquish them.

As the facilitator, you're responsible for monitoring the activity of the groups. It's easy to sit back and watch the clock instead of moving from group to group and helping them out if they're struggling. The participants may be the experts in terms of what they're designing and what context they're designing it for, but you're the expert in guiding them through the activities.

When to avoid participatory design

There are times when your Spider-Sense may go off and warn you that something may not be right. Participatory design is a great method when it's used correctly, but there are times when a different approach may be better.

If you are approached to give the impression that participatory design is taking place, but it's simply a guise for someone else attempting to sell an idea, you may want to consider stepping away. The premise behind participatory design is that others are involved because they have skin in the game, and the design being accurate helps meet all of their needs in some capacity. When you strip that away, the activity may do more harm than good, and as a facilitator this could put you in a position of questionable ethics and morality.

There are also times where problems may be better solved in isolation. Prior to taking part in participatory design, or as part of a larger design workshop, you may want to have people work on their own and review the designs that they've come up with.

The power of many

With participatory design, you bring together diverse groups of people and help them work together to design the best possible product, service, or other solution. It can be a challenge, but also very rewarding! You may get to observe, as Sunni Brown puts it, "an awakening" that occurs in members of the group as they learn that there are a variety of ways to work toward solutions that don't involve long, boring meetings and overloaded email threads. The participants start to see other opportunities where participatory design activities can be useful in the work that they're doing, and they open themselves up to working and operating in new ways.

During participatory design activities, participants have permission to do things they wouldn't normally do in their day-to-day roles; you open the door to new, liberating ways of thinking and tackling problems. You may help the groups uncover new leaders and provide new opportunities for people who can thrive in participatory design activities that are different from their daily routines.

Participatory design is your opportunity to unlock solutions that might take rounds and rounds of iterations and partial successes to achieve.

Section 3

One-on-One Facilitation

Any meeting with another person provides you the opportunity to change the way you view a project, product, topic, or the world through conversation. By being aware of the different types of one-on-one facilitation you may encounter, you can keep yourself focused on the information you seek.

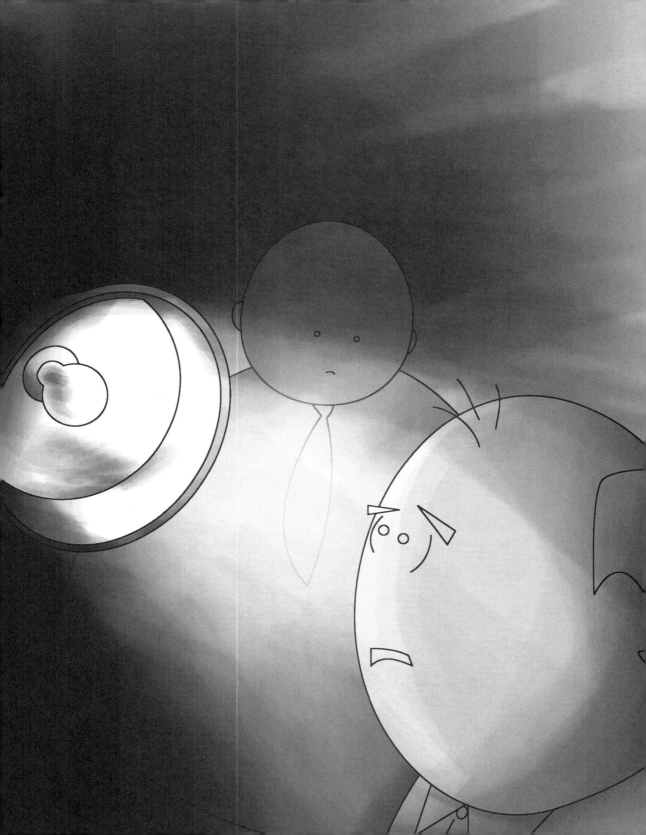

Chapter 11

Interviews

I've never learned anything while I was talking.

— Larry King

Sitting down and having a conversation with a person offers a unique opportunity to learn about his or her personal story. This story is not something everyone gets to hear; it's a true gift that can affect your project, career, or personal life. Interviews can occur at any time, but most are scheduled events where someone has agreed to meet with you and hopefully share information with you. How you facilitate an interview is what determines how personal you can get with your questions and, more importantly, how much information you will gather. No question is ever inappropriate, but when you ask it and how you ask it can be all that separates you from gaining the understanding you want and leaving empty-handed.

Types of interviews

The type of information you're hoping to gather differs based on the type of interview you're conducting. Some interviews get you to a deep personal experience a person has had, and others allow you to learn more about a specific task they perform. The end goal of the interview dictates the type of interview you conduct: contextual inquiry, stakeholder interview, customer/user interview, or job interview.

Contextual inquiry

If your goal is to gain a deep understanding of how a person, or a group of people, does a job or attempts to accomplish a particular objective, a contextual inquiry is the best method to use. When you perform a contextual inquiry, focus your questions on the actions and behaviors you observe directly. Don't be a distraction to the participant; any interruptions to the interviewee's normal workflow should be related to that workflow. This is an activity based on active listening skills, paying attention to details, and learning more about the participant.

Stakeholder interview

To better understand the history, context, and domain of a topic as it relates to a new project, you'll find yourself interviewing various stakeholders. These conversations tend to last between 30 and 60 minutes, where all the topics discussed relate to the project you're assigned to. Since project stakeholders can have many responsibilities and may have tight schedules, it's important to structure each interview to hit as many key areas as possible without prolonging the conversation. At the end of the interview, ask the stakeholder if there is time for a follow-up interview to continue the discussion or discuss additional topics that you were not able to cover. If they found value in the time they spent with you, they will likely agree.

Customer/user interview

In the design profession, the best source of information about how an application should behave or how it should be designed can be determined by interviewing the people who actually use the application. These interviews focus on how someone uses an existing product or solution, or may use a proposed one. These interviews can last a long time, depending on the type of product or service that needs to be designed, or redesigned. During the interview, you want to learn about pain points, workarounds, and general expectations on interactive behavior. Users of products and services are a wealth of information, and can be more than willing to work with you to cover all topics related to the existing product.

Job interview

A job interview is interesting because you have a participant who's trying to sell himself, and you're trying to assess his skills and personality. The goal of a job interview is a simple one. As an interviewer, you want to understand why the applicant feels he is right for the job and determine if he'll be a good fit with your team culturally. The participant is also conducting his own interview with you: trying to determine whether your team's culture is right for him and the work your team does is attractive. Job interviews are all about determining if a match can be made between the applicant and the hiring company. Both parties need to draw their own conclusions by asking their own questions.

Prepare for your interviews

The facilitation of interviews begins when you start to think about the topics you want to cover and the questions you'll need to ask to learn about those topics. You may find yourself having fictional conversations in your head as you figure out the right flow and method to take.

Guide your way through an interview

An interview guide is the most reliable tool to help you get through an interview. This guide is a catalog of all the topics you want to cover and the type of questions to ask. Don't think of the guide as a script; this makes the interview come across as prescriptive and makes it hard to be conversational. Prior to the interview, have teammates, project managers, project sponsors, the hiring manager, or a handy friend review the guide to validate your thinking. Feedback collected on the guide will help you refine it and prepare for the interview.

Limit your topic areas

Every interview should focus on a small set of topics. A common mistake made when performing interviews for the first time is taking on too many topics in a single session. Too many topics can scatter the focus of the interview, and that reduces the amount of time you get with each topic.

Any given interview should focus on two to four topics, depending on the complexity. If there are more topics you know you'll need to cover, schedule additional interviews with the participants. If the participants feel like their voice is being heard and their time is being used wisely, they are more likely to make time to meet with you on multiple occasions.

Plan out the talking points

Since interviews are a tool to understand a person's past experiences and knowledge about a specific topic, it's a good tactic to plan out an interview like a story, similar to how you plan a workshop as discussed in Chapter 7, "Workshops." Act I is when you ask the initial questions that give you an introduction to the participant. Act II consists of questions reserved for learning the experiences and habits of the participant. Act III is the closing of the interview where the risky questions get asked. Each act can be planned to cover specific talking points and topics.

By breaking the interview into these content chunks, you can practice the flow of the interview beforehand by yourself or with a volunteer doing some role-playing. When transitioning from one act to another, identify topics and questions that make this a natural and smooth transition. This adds fluidity and rhythm to your conversations, which strengthens the conversational tone you want to achieve. **Table 11.1** shows an example structure for an interview guide.

Improv your written questions

Prior to conducting any interviews, when you are planning out the topics you want to learn about, you're going to be writing down a lot of potential questions. Each of these questions is meant to help you learn more about another person's life, job, or personal knowledge, but not every question is for everyone.

When conducting an interview, each question you created during the planning should remind you of the purpose of that question. Based on the purpose, phrase the question in a way that best works for the participant you're working with at the time. Every question can be asked in a number of ways to get you to the same type of answer. Use this flexibility to your advantage to tailor your questions to the individual, without forgetting the underlying goal of a specific line of questioning.

Go off the reservation

Your interview guide is just that, a guide. Based on the conversation you actually have with a participant, additional questions may be required that take you away from the original plan you laid out in your interview guide. Feel free to do this from time to time, as long as you don't sacrifice other conversation points you know you need to reach. As you perform more interviews, you'll find that occasionally the best questions you can ask are those you didn't think of when you were writing your guide.

Amend your interviews

You will eventually have to go back to your interview guide for updates or restructuring. As the interviews progress, you'll learn what works and what doesn't, and which questions result in the most profound information. The changes to your plan will include updating or rephrasing your existing questions, adding or removing questions, and moving questions to different points of the interview.

TABLE 11.1 Example Structure of Interview Guide

SECTION	DESCRIPTION
Note to Reader and Reviewers	Provide context and background for people unfamiliar with an interviewing process or the project.
Introduction	Scripted introduction that is read to the interviewee speaks to the scope of the interview and any special topics that need to be covered before the interview begins, such as needing to see personal medical records.
Review Recruiting Information	Quick review of the information you collected about the participant during the recruitment phase to check for accuracy and updates.
Day in the Life	Questions that relate to the participant's typical day at work or at home. This conversation piece is meant to get the participant used to talking to you and comfortable with the interview setup.
Personal Information	Discussion points that cover the participant demographics, experience, and background. This will provide you with possible areas of focus to ask about later on in the interview process.
Topic Questions	Groups of questions that focus on a specific topic area, where initial questions are fairly high level and move toward more detailed questions. It is common to have a small set of topic areas you want to cover.
Task-Based Questions	Occasionally, interviews will move past being conversational and focus on typical tasks the participants accomplishes. This section allows you to ask the participant to observe these tasks and learn how and why they exhibit certain behaviors.
Wrap-up	A quick conversation that covers how the information collected during the interview will be used and any information on renumeration or additional follow-ups.
High-Level Thoughts and Reactions	This section is for you to make any notes on your general thoughts, feelings, or reactions about the interview. These should be documented following every interview.
Environmental Notes	If the interview occurred at someone's house or personal office, interesting aspects of the participant's environment should be noted here.

Iterate on your questions

During the first few interviews you conduct on a new project, you'll be relying on the knowledge you had prior to the interviews to craft your questions. As you learn more, it's natural to go back and modify or add questions you want to ask future participants. The initial group of participants will always be guinea pigs to test how well you prepared the talking points and questions. The first few interviews will tell you whether or not a topic area is important, and you may learn about new topics that should be explored with other participants. The questions you plan to ask will mature as you learn what works and what does not.

It's important to keep the core questions you need to ask the same so you can go back after the interviews have been conducted and do proper comparisons. If all of your interviews have completely different questions, then you'll run into issues when analyzing for patterns and overall findings. Iterate on questions that allow you to explore different aspects or points of view of the core questions you'll be asking to get to information that might be buried below the surface.

Save the best questions for last

The questions that have some of the biggest payoffs are the riskiest to ask. If the participant does not feel comfortable answering or gives vague, empty answers, it's a sign that the risk did not pay off. This can result in the interview being cut short, or future answers being short and shallow. Since this is always possible, save your riskier questions for the last part of the interview. By doing this, you ensure that the other information collected before you pull out the risky question was collected in a more comfortable scenario. No matter what, don't be afraid to ask the risky question. If the risk pays off, you end up with some of the richest, most valuable content you could ask for.

Conducting your interviews

Now is the time to sit down face-to-face, or phone-to-phone, and conduct the actual interview. This is the point where your goal is to create a friendly, conversational environment.

Conversations vs. interrogations

When conducting your first few interviews, the worst thing you can do is interrogate the participant by sticking to the questions you have planned out. This a common mistake with novice interviewers, but over time you learn to avoid the interrogation model and adopt more of a conversational one. All interviews aim to reach a goal where you learn more about a topic by encouraging participants to share information with you. This topic could be about the job, the applications the participants use, or about themselves. How you present yourself and how you ask the questions is what allows you to learn more about that topic.

No one likes being interrogated, but people typically enjoy being part of a conversation. This is especially true when the conversation revolves around those you're interviewing. As Dale Carnegie says in *How to Win Friends and Influence People* (Pocket Books, 1998):

> **Let the other person do a great deal of the talking.**

The one thing most people enjoy talking about is—you guessed it—themselves! People like to share their accomplishments and experiences, and if you've built a strong enough relationship with them, they may even share some of their failures. You can accomplish this by asking questions that are natural and that feel like they're part of a larger conversation.

Qualities of natural questions

- Easy to answer: The participant can easily relate to the question and provide an answer for it.

- Nonoffensive: The question does not touch on any potentially harmful or inappropriate topics.

- Nonexclusive: For the context of the question, anyone would be able to provide some type of response.

- Responses are nonjudgmental: The answer will not lead to you, or any others present, judging the participant.

Know when to stop digging

There always comes a point when the participant is done talking about a topic. This can happen for a number of reasons—perhaps the participant has exhausted his or her knowledge around a topic or doesn't trust you enough to give you the information you're asking for. If you continue to hammer away at a participant because you think there might be more information there, you'll get to the point where you run the risk of doing more harm than good. Future questions and conversation areas will suffer, as the interviewee may begin to put up barriers as "protection" from your questions. One of the worst perceptions a participant can have of you is being pushy and attempting to gain information that does not exist or that he or she does not want to give up.

We tend to run away from an interviewer that is asking too many questions.

Following are some signs that indicate it may be time to move on to a new topic:

- Defensive body language: People tend take on closed postures when they're done talking about a topic. (See Chapter 4, "Preparing for Personalities," for examples.)

- Hesitation: Extended pauses when responding to a line of questioning could be a sign that you've reached the depth of the participant's knowledge on the topic or that he or she is unwilling to share the information you're looking for.

- Off-topic responses: Answering a question with an answer that does not relate to the question asked is typically an act of avoidance. The participant is avoiding giving an answer, or does not know what to say, and so attempts to change the topic.

Your goal is to create an open and friendly relationship, and if a participant does not want to share something, you can either let it go or revisit the topic once he or she has opened up a bit more.

Get personal

The start of an interview is very much like the beginning of a first date. You and the participant are getting to know each other's personalities, physical behaviors, and trying to get a better sense of who the other person is. This naturally means the opening line of questions should be fairly open-ended and not try to get to information that could be too personal. As the interview progresses and you both learn more about the other, it's possible for the conversation to become more personal. This is a magical moment, because the participant has let you into his private personal space and made himself vulnerable. By getting to this point, you may start to learn what makes the participant tick and collect the type of information that can lead to insights.

Whoa, that was unexpected

Interviews can be fun and interesting because of the unique personalities involved. But with unique personalities sometimes come uncomfortable situations and surprising findings. Regardless of what happens, it's important to the flow of the interview that you act normally and do not show surprise. Showing surprise, either verbally or with body language, can cause enough damage to the interview that any information you gather could be invalid or not trustworthy because the participant goes on the defensive for the rest of the session. It's best to simply take it in and move on to the next topic area or question.

Build on established trust

Trust is the most valuable commodity when you're doing an interview. Trust does not come easily—it's something that must be earned. From the moment you begin the interview, each question you ask either helps to build the trust between you and the participant or challenges the trust you have already established. Think about trust as a bank account: be sure you have a large enough balance that the personal questions you need to ask can be paid for. This is true for any type of interview, and especially important for sessions that take place in a person's personal space, such as the home.

An interviewer taking a deposit out of a "trust" to cash in for a question.

Meet the Expert: Dana Chisnell

Dana Chisnell is a methodology nerd and civic design wonk for the research firm she founded, UsabilityWorks. She explores the intersections among design, language, context, and human behavior, and is often surprised by what she sees.

•

Why is it so important to control how you react to surprising comments or situations when interviewing a participant?

1. The participant might think you're being judgmental. As a result, the person may shut down.

2. You can influence how *the participant* reacts.

3. The session isn't about you. It's about the participant and how he or she interacts with a design. As the moderator, you are but a vessel for data.

What was your most interesting experience and how did you react to it?

Just the other day, I was interviewing a couple in a field study in which I was trying to learn about the mental model people have of "retirement." One of the questions in the script was, "What are the three most challenging things you've ever been through in your life, and how did you handle them?" One of the participants told me about joining the Army during the Vietnam War, expecting to ride it out with a desk job stateside. But he was deployed early on as an "advisor" and nearly as soon as he and his platoon arrived, they were attacked. He was shot through the chest, very near his heart. He said he'd never talked about it before. I don't know why he talked about it in this session.

I wanted to cry, and I very nearly did. Instead, I thanked him for telling his story. Hearing stories like that was important to my understanding of where people came from and what their worldviews were. I did cry when I got home.

It's not the first time that's happened. I've done studies with people who were recently diagnosed with serious health issues. They're sometimes angry, sometimes depressed, sometimes lost, sometimes all three and more.

I've also had people cry in my sessions—well, only twice in 30 years. The first was a young woman who was so anxious about her performance that she broke down. We took a break, and I soothed her somewhat. Of course I told her that this was not a test of her, but she was helping me learn about the usability of the design (this must have been about 1999). But she couldn't go on.

The second episode of crying happened in a study a couple of years ago. I was testing a retirement calculation wizard. Part of the wizard was choosing goals and setting priorities. Most of the goals are happy things—learn a language, start a business, travel—but some are about personal duty, such as caring for aging parents. This person got to the one about caring for aging parents and started to sob. Turns out her mother had been diagnosed with ALS a few months before and it was quite advanced. She realized she'd never have a chance to take care of her mother the way her mother had taken care of her. We stopped, of course, and turned off all the recording equipment. I asked her if she had a cell phone. She said yes, so I asked her if there was someone she wanted to call, and I got her a glass of water. She said she wanted to talk to her father, but wouldn't call him because she didn't want to interrupt him at work. After a few minutes, we went back to the session because she wanted to, even though we told her we'd give her the honorarium and get her a cab and she could go right then.

But there was this one time—I don't even remember what the usability test was for anymore. At the end of the session, I asked a male participant what was missing from the site. He said, "All Britney Spears, all the time." All I could do was crack up.

What tactics do you find useful for building and maintaining trust over the course of an interview?

Set expectations from the beginning: why we're here, what you're going to do, what you expect of the participant, how long we'll be in the session, etc.

Remind the participants that they're helping you design something.

Laugh when they say something funny. You can be human and still be open and objective.

Appeal to their wisdom, expertise, or experience.

How do you know a participant is ready for you to start asking personal questions? What are some signs that you look for?

On the study about the mental model of "retirement," there's a lot of talk about money and personal identity. This can be awkward for some people. I call them before the session and tell them, "I'm going to ask a lot of questions about money, and what you value about working (or not working). I will not ask your net worth or about specific amounts of anything. If there are things you don't want to answer, you don't have to."

So, I give them the option to not answer questions. I apologize sometimes before asking: "I'm sorry to ask this…" or "If this feels like I'm prying, you don't have to say, but…" or "It would help me to know, but you don't have to answer.…"

Signs that they're ready to answer?

They seem engaged in the conversation, and they're relaxed about talking about themselves.

They've been sharing their experiences pretty freely already.

Also, remember that we've usually had a conversation between screening and the session. So when I walk into their home, or when we meet in the lab, I'm not a perfect stranger.

Learn about people's stories

One of the jobs of an interviewer is to collect stories. After the opening round of questions, everything asked should get the participant to tell you a story. Some stories will be longer than others, and you'll need to control the flow enough to be able to move on if need be, based on your time constraints for the interview.

As a person tells you more and more personal information, it's natural for him or her to progressively begin to trust you. As this trust builds, it lets you ask more risky questions. If you're attempting to learn about a person's financial habits, don't ask to see financial records at the start of the interview. Wait until the participant is comfortable with you and knows that you would never betray a trust.

Use active listening skills

One thing every interviewer needs is great listening ears and the ability to actively listen for a long period of time. It's not enough to simply take note of what people tell you and the stories they share—you have to be able to tie together what they say. Pay attention to opportunities to bring up something a participant said earlier in the conversation to provide more context or detail around the current topic.

Paying close attention to what's being said and how it relates shows the participant that you're really listening. This seems obvious, but many people are used to being interviewed by someone who acts more like a recorder than an actively engaged interviewer. Showing participants that you're the latter keeps them engaged and shows that their input is valued and appreciated.

When you refer to previous points and insights, you also open up the possibility for the participant to go a bit deeper and provide additional information. Earlier in the interview, the person may not have been willing to share information with you when it was brought up for whatever reason. The chance to revisit an old point gives both you and the participant a chance to take a mental breather, offering a break from discussing new topics.

Final thoughts on interviews

Questions that you did not write yourself can sometimes come off as unnatural and the participant may be able to pick up on this. That's why this chapter has focused on the need to create and maintain a conversational tone when conducting an interview. You can thoroughly plan out what you want to talk about and how you want to talk about it, but the best interviews are those that don't feel like interviews at all. The information that gets shared by the participant comes out naturally and makes the overall interview flow smoother. Always aim to maintain a certain amount of flow and openness with your interviews; if you do this, your participants will thank you for not badgering them for answers to your questions.

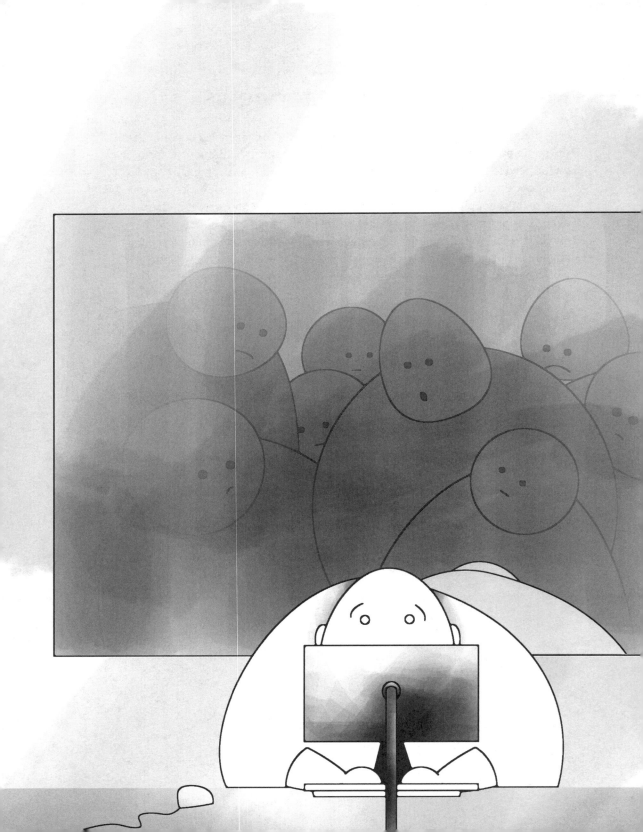

Chapter 12

Usability Testing

Whatever your team might call it—usability testing, design testing, getting feedback—the most effective input for informed design decisions is data about the behavior and performance of people using a design to reach their own goals.
— Dana Chisnell

The best usability testing is done when you get to observe a user performing tasks. The best seat in the house for usability testing is that of the moderator—you get to work closely with users and watch their actions firsthand. You also have the responsibility of guiding them through the session and all their tasks. The art of facilitating is important in usability testing; you need to be calm and confident and put your participants at ease. Preparation and practice will help you when it comes time to talk to users, and over time you'll find the style that works best for you, making it easier for you to slip into this role.

Types of usability testing

Usability testing falls into one of three primary categories: in-person testing, remote moderated testing, and remote unmoderated testing. You may find it easier to think of as having a facilitator present or being handled by proxy through technology. The information you can collect from verbal and nonverbal responses by moderating in person is a great deal more qualitative. And, unlike unmoderated testing, it provides you with much more context than data points or screen recordings (if available). As with all things, the method you choose will largely be determined by the amount of time and resources you have available, so make sure you choose wisely.

In-person testing

In-person testing involves some very basic elements: you, the facilitator; a user who will perform tasks that you provide; and something to test. In most cases, you'll have cameras recording the user from multiple angles, screen-recording software on a laptop to capture everything the user does, and a one-way mirror through which observers and note takers dutifully snacking away on M&Ms or other snacks. However, given the more cost-effective and portable nature of technology today, the primary purpose of an in-person usability test is to observe a user performing tasks via an interface. Additionally, you want to learn from the user's physical, emotional, and verbal reactions to various tasks. The reactions you observe will help you decide whether or not to probe for additional information from the user or allow him or her to continue on to more tasks.

Remote moderated testing

Thanks largely to advances in technology, usability testing can be performed almost anywhere you can find space for a laptop. This is a good thing, because it's quite possible that you'll need to conduct usability testing with your participant from a remote location. There are many tools that allow you to share and record a participant's screen activity while talking to him or her through a recorded phone conference or voice over IP (VoIP) sessions.

As a facilitator, it's incredibly important that you keep participants focused on the tasks at hand and engaged in "thinking aloud" to compensate for the missing nonverbal cues you would normally see if you were administering the test in person.

You can also keep them engaged through continual feedback, offering affirmations and acknowledgement of their actions, and nudging them along through their tasks, without providing inappropriate guidance.

Remote moderated testing should not be considered a replacement for in-person testing, but it's an alternative approach when time and resources are limited. For more information, check out *Remote Research: Real Users, Real Time, Real Research* by Nate Bolt and Tony Tulathimutte (Rosenfeld Media, 2010).

Unmoderated remote testing

One way to reach a large number of participants over a given period of time is to perform unmoderated remote testing. The gist of this is that you create your test environment—be it static screens, an interactive prototype, or a fully functional website or application—and provide clear instructions to participants as to the tasks you wish them to perform.

This may sound fairly simple, but special rigor must be applied to the scenario you've created. As a facilitator, you need to make sure that you're providing explicit instructions to your participants, and that they're able to follow them and accomplish them. You will not be present; there will be no nonverbal cues to read and no thinking aloud to react to, so you have to ensure that your instructions will get you the feedback you're seeking. Make sure that you perform at least one thorough test run with a sampling of participants prior to running your first live test so you can update and improve your tasks prior to launching a live unmoderated test.

The upside to unmoderated remote testing beyond travel and resources costs is that you can turn it on and continue to work on other things while the test runs. You can capture as much data as you like over a period of time, a limited number of participants, or some other metric that you determine (X answers to a specific question, X answers of Y to a specific question, and so forth) without needing to be present while it happens.

You will, of course, miss all the nonverbal cues and any thinking aloud that participants would normally do during in-person scenarios. Your data will mostly be quantitative, based on the specific tasks that you asked your participants to perform and that may not provide you with the same level of insight that in-person testing affords.

Test planning

Usability testing requires a lot of coordination, because many activities need to happen prior to the test. Aside from the various approvals and recruiting, you still need to plan for what will occur during the time allotted for your usability tests. Your planning should include all the steps necessary during the course of the test, from room setup to the setup and closing of each individual session, and everything in between.

Testing scripts (plan for the session)

Testing scripts are your guide, nay, your sherpa through the wilderness of the usability test. When you plan scripts correctly, they ensure that you can easily hit all the information points you need to convey to your participants and keep you in the flow of the session.

A typical usability testing script may include the following: consent to record the session, an introduction to the test, some background or preliminary questions, a scenario description, the tasks, and test completion information. This goes beyond an outline; you're writing the actual script for these sections and allowing others to review them to make sure you're being accurate in your language, legally compliant, and sticking to an agreed-upon plan. As a facilitator, it's your job to make sure that you've provided the right amount of detail so you can follow it easily and remain focused.

The **consent to record** grants permission to you from your participants to record the session under whatever rules and guidelines you have provided to them. In general, these allow participants to feel safe about the usage of the recording, which is frequently used only for revisiting and notetaking by team members. Obtaining writing consent is ideal, but some legal departments may let you accept verbal consent if you're not in person and have the consent recorded.

The **test introduction** sets the stage for the usability test. This is where you thank your participants and explain to them what a usability test is, what they will be reviewing, and what you expect from them throughout the course of the usability test.

You may ask **preliminary questions** that help you understand more of the participants' background than was provided through a screener. You may also choose to ask additional questions around the topic of the task, for example, if you're testing a movie theater website, how frequently do the participants go to movies? Do they purchase tickets online or at the theater? How frequently do they use the Internet? These can help establish how you adjust your approach to the participants, as you can get a basic understanding of their general context to the tasks in your test.

The **scenario description** provides more detailed background about the usability test itself and the focus of the tasks.

The **tasks** contain stage cues, such as unspoken facilitator directions and instructions to help set up the task, as well as the actual tasks, goals, and potential issues to explore. You may want to provide such information as "start with page x" before a task to help guide the testing.

At **test completion,** you'll want to clearly thank the participants for their time and explain any incentive information, including how and when this will be taken care of if it's not immediately and in person, as well as collect and confirm any pertinent information for disbursing the incentive. It's good practice to provide your contact information to allow participants' to follow up if they have any post-testing questions or concerns.

What makes a good task?

One of the biggest challenges you may have when planning a usability test is crafting a really good quality task. Phrasing and context are essential when you present the task to a participant. This is difficult enough in person or when speaking to the participant directly, and when performing unmoderated testing it can be almost impossible to predict how a participant will interpret your written tasks, so it's important to know how create that good task.

There is a balancing act involved in creating tasks; you want to make sure that you're explicit and clear, but you also need to make sure that participants are given enough information and context that they are able to predict the expected outcome of the task. At the same time, you want to avoid being overly vague and ambiguous to the point where participants become lost or frustrated about what they're supposed to accomplish.

Some basic guidelines to follow when creating usability testing tasks are:

- Identify the primary tasks a user would typically perform when using the application. Include some tasks that are representative of high-value or high-frequency tasks outside the primary set.

- Avoid using terms that relate directly to labels found within the application being evaluated. If you want your participants to submit a form and the call-to-action on the form is "submit," think of a way to ask your question without using the word "submit."

- Focus on the goal that the participant is attempting to accomplish with a task. What answers are they trying to find? What is the user's goal when performing the task?

- Keep tasks as simple as possible so you don't overwhelm the participant with too many actions. If the task you're hoping to observe is significant, break it into subtasks to make it more manageable for the participant.

- After you've created the tasks, review them with another team member or other party who is not as close to them as you are. When you seek out feedback from others, you can uncover ambiguities or other instructions that may be overly complex or unclear.

By following these guidelines, you'll be on your way to ensuring that your tasks are clearly actionable by your participants. When in doubt, an extra round of practice will help you iron out any wrinkles in your tasks.

Sample task

Task 1: Create a new online account.

(Read to participant)

You've received your bill from Acme Utilities in the mail, and you've decided that you want to manage your account and payments online. Using the web browser, access the Acme Utilities website and create a new online account for yourself.

Dry runs make perfect

Prior to the first day of testing, you should perform at least one dry run with internal participants. This is no different than other types of facilitation—the more prepared you are, the more comfortable you'll be, and that will be very obvious to your participants.

The more comfortable and at ease your participants are, the more likely they are to think aloud and share information with you as you go through the tasks with them. Do yourself, your client or team, and the participants a favor and rehearse until you're comfortable with the material. Even better, rehearse with real people who can relate to the application being tested, even if they're not in your actual participant pool. You may be surprised at what you uncover and how much better prepared you'll feel just by putting a single, non-recruited participant through the usability test in its entirety.

On each day of the testing, make sure that all of your technology is set up and ready to go, and set up your dial-in and any other tools for testing. If possible, perform an abbreviated dry run to make sure you're prepared and ready to go. Once that's taken care of, it's time to start to facilitate with your participants.

Proctoring the usability test

Once your participants show up for a usability test by dialing in to an online session or you've been called to escort them into the lab, conference room, or office that's being used as the observation room, you have formally begun facilitating the session. This typically involves some small talk as you get things started, and you help make the participants comfortable with you, while at the same time learning a bit more about them, how they respond to your questions, and their general attitude and comfort. You can learn a lot about someone during this time that will inform how smoothly the usability test will go and alert you to any personality issues you may need to deal with.

Introducing the test

The test introduction is essentially the script that explains to the participants what will take place during the session and what your expectations of them are. This is the opportunity to thank them for participating, remind them to think their thoughts out loud, and remind them that you're not testing them, but rather the application, website, or device. In addition, by utilizing the same script for each participant, you ensure that all of your participants get the same information about the session.

Preliminary questions

In most cases, the preliminary questions are optional. Some people use these as an opportunity to warm up participants to the tasks ahead. Some use them as an opportunity to get additional demographics on the participants. Others may use this as an opportunity to get additional information (including a case of running quick A/B preferences on visual design concepts).

Task presentation

There are different ways to approach presenting tasks to your participants. The most common way is to read them the task and let them set off performing it. In some cases, you may need to repeat the task in order to help the participants become comfortable and clear as to what it is they're attempting to accomplish. It's important that you stick to your script—a lot of time and effort was expended to carefully craft the tasks—and not take liberties when describing a task so you don't inadvertently guide them toward an outcome.

You can also have participants read the task, preferably aloud, to familiarize them with it and prompt any questions for clarification, if needed. Consider your responses to participant questions carefully so you don't provide any direction toward completing the task, but instead focus on the intention and purpose of the question itself. You may also want to ask the participants what they think the question means and nudge them toward performing and completing the task while thinking aloud.

Taskus interruptus

There may be times during a moderated usability test that you need to interrupt the participants. Consider these times carefully and be confident that the interruption will not distract them from their current task. Your interruption should happen only when you require additional information or a deeper understanding as to why a participant took a particular action, or what occurred during the test that was different from the participants' expectations. Sometimes participants may reach a dead end, or feel unable to complete a task, and you may need to interject to find a way to help move them along. As sessions are likely to occur in a finite amount of time, you have to be prepared to help move them along and make decisions to ensure that you're able to accomplish all, or at least as much as possible, given the allotted time.

Some potential scenarios for interrupting usability tests are:

- **Getting past technical issues.** Technical issues normally come up when you're evaluating a prototype or beta application. It's best to not give the technical problem much attention; just inform participants why the issue came up and then encourage them to move on.

- **Working through roadblocks.** Participants aren't always able to complete a task on their own. Occasionally, they need your assistance to get past a step in the process or find the required functionality. Avoid giving participants direct instruction as much as possible, and instead ask questions that naturally lead them toward the right path or help provide attention to the correct area on the interface.

- **Answering inquiring questions.** One of the main things you want to avoid during a usability study is getting into a question-and-answer loop with a participant. It's important to keep the participant engaged in the task and thinking aloud, and refrain from providing information that can lead the participant toward a biased result. The best way to avoid this trap is by getting into the habit of answering a question with another question, and asking what the participant thinks should happen in response to the question is a simple way to do that.

- **Learning more about a participant's reaction.** The best justification for an interruption is to learn more about a participant's reaction to what he or she is viewing, or an action that he or she just took. When something unexpected happens, a participant can communicate this to you both verbally and nonverbally. When you recognize these cues, it's an opportunity to interrupt and ask for more details about what the participant is thinking or what he or she was expecting to have happened.

Building participants' confidence

Some participants may not feel qualified, for one reason or another, to take part in a usability test. They may not even understand why they have been chosen to take part in it. Part of your job as a facilitator is to help them through these negative thoughts and guide them into participating.

You may hear responses like, "I'm sorry I'm not giving you the information you're looking for" or "I'm sorry if I'm not being very helpful," which should be viewed as opportunities to further explain and reinforce that all information is good information, and that the participant is not being tested, but the design is. Participants need to understand that their insight is helping to drive improvements and enhancements that can make it better.

You may also want to take time to explain how the recruiting process was organized, and how participants were selected so that they understand that they're being useful and helpful, and that they've been chosen to help for a reason, and as representatives of a number of users—not just themselves. This can help the participant feel special and important, and help your usability test to continue.

Collecting responses to the testing

If you're facilitating an in-person usability test, you should not be the person collecting the responses; you'll need to focus on guiding the participants through the tasks and providing them with the necessary feedback without distracting them. You should have ample recording equipment and additional dedicated resources that will assist with collecting data points. In some scenarios, you may be required to revisit the recordings of the sessions and take notes yourself, but that's not really the most efficient approach.

If you're performing moderated remote testing, you may be required to collect responses during the test, and it's easy for this to become distracting. There are many different approaches to being successful in this, but the best approach is to record everything and have enough additional resources to help recording data points as you go. Remember, participants can still hear you and any background noise you may add by typing or writing. It's difficult for anyone to focus on more than one thing at a time, and participants may pick up on your lack of focus on them and their tasks.

Closing out the session

When you've reached the end of the tasks that you have for your participants, discreetly check with any additional observers to find out if there are any additional questions that should be asked prior to wrapping up. This allows your observers to play an additional role in the usability test, and ensures that you haven't overlooked anything valuable from the participants while you were facilitating.

After checking with your observers, give the participants the opportunity to ask any outstanding questions that they may have and offer more detailed answers. You may have purposefully avoided some of their questions during the session to learn how they would handle the task, and now is the time to give them additional information if they request it. Feel free to disclose as much as you're allowed to share based on the restrictions or legal terms of the usability test.

This is also another opportunity to re-establish that the purpose of the usability test is to learn how people interact with the system by testing it with real users, and that the participants were not being evaluated.

Handling incentives

Once the session is complete, you'll need to make good on any incentive that you may have offered. If you're providing incentives digitally, such as PayPal or Amazon gift certificates, you can collect and verify email addresses from your participants and send those along right after the session, if you're able to do so. Otherwise, it's OK to inform the participants that you'll send incentives upon completion of the testing sessions as a whole (it can be easier to send incentives en masse), but don't miss your promised delivery date!

As an act of good faith, consider sharing your professional contact information with the participants, if it's allowed, so they can feel free to follow up with any questions, concerns, or issues with the incentive.

Additional resources

Usability testing is a great way to learn more about how users interact with a system. This chapter provides you with a lot of important information for you, as the facilitator, but only scratches the surface on the topic as a whole.

There are a great number of resources that can help you learn much more about usability testing, such as:

- *Handbook of Usability Testing* by Jeffrey Rubin and Dana Chisnell (Wiley, 2008)

- *Remote Research: Real Users, Real Time, Real Research* by Nate Bolt and Tony Tulathimutte (Rosenfeld, 2010)

- *Don't Make Me Think* by Steve Krug (New Riders, 2005)

- *Rocket Surgery Made Easy* by Steve Krug (New Riders, 2009)

- *A Practical Guide to Usability Testing* by Joseph S. Dumas and Janice C. Redish (Intellect Ltd., 1999)

- User Interface Engineering's online articles (www.uie.com/browse/usability_testing)

Chapter 13

Sales Calls

Nobody likes to be sold, but everybody likes to buy.
— Jeffrey Gitomer

You probably do not sell used cars. You may or may not consider yourself a salesperson, but if you have clients, or want them, then you're involved in the sales process. And whatever your role in that process, you'd probably bristle at any association between what you do and the work of salesmen as portrayed in fiction over the last couple of centuries.

Folk stories of unscrupulous peddlers in New England are as old as the United States. In the nineteenth century, traveling snake oil salesmen showed up in Mark Twain's writing. When playwright Arthur Miller wanted to dramatize the dark side of America's industrial success after World War II, he made his main character a struggling salesman. *Death of a Salesman*'s Willy Loman takes pride in being well liked, but fails because he offers little else to his customers.

The salespeople on television are walking punch lines with slippery ethics and questionable tastes. We've had obnoxious Herb Tarlek (*WKRP in Cincinnati*), frustrated Al Bundy (*Married...with Children*), and, most recently, bizarre Dwight Schrute (*The Office*). Luckily, you're not selling what any of these shady characters sold.

Based on your interest in this book, you're probably involved in the sale of services. If you build things, or define things, or in other ways share expertise with clients, you don't really have much in common with the popular stereotype of a salesperson. As a result, you're free to change the way you think and talk about the entire sales process.

Redefining the sales call

The sales call is an opportunity, not just for you, but for the client as well. Both sides can benefit by treating it as a first phase (for new clients) or an important *next* phase (for existing clients) in the relationship. The sales call should be more of an initial investigation than a dramatic performance: The client has specific needs and you have specific value. How well the two intersect defines the potential long-term success of the relationship.

Karen McGrane, managing partner at Bond Art and Science, has two or three phone calls a week with existing and potential clients:

> **There's a sense that you're going to be a slick, oily, sharkskin-suited used car salesman. The truth of it is that sales is a genuine conversation to find out whether you're the right fit. I personally believe that for the most positive sales that you do, you don't really have to persuade anyone of anything. Instead, it's just an honest conversation about what they need and what you can deliver.**

Focus on defining and solving the client's problem, even if your organization turns out not to be the best solution. If that sounds crazy, then this will sound worse: The purpose of a sales call is not always to make a sale.

When you concentrate on helping clients get to where they want to be, you learn more about their organization than you ever can when you're distracted by the money. They may offer up insightful information about their capabilities, their strengths and weaknesses, and their vision for the future—data you can rarely glean from the outside.

A good client will recognize the integrity of your approach, which can lead to your organization playing a larger role than just a single project. Not all clients live up to this higher standard for a sales call. If while you focus on creating solutions, it feels like all the client tries to do is get a lower price for your services, then you gain a vital glimpse of how poorly the project may go. Those kinds of insights shouldn't be ignored. As McGrane says:

> The situations that I have regretted most in my career are situations where I had a bad feeling right from the start, but I took something on because I thought the money would be good or because I thought it would look good in my portfolio or because I thought maybe if we got through this initial hump where I was getting a bad vibe from the client, maybe things would work out later and maybe it would become a great relationship.
>
> Those things don't usually work out and those have tended to be the situations where I find myself in an unproductive, unhealthy client relationship where I don't make any money and I really kind of hate my life.

Fight the urge to spend 45 minutes talking about your value or your work for past clients. Instead, turn the conversation into a problem-solving exercise and your actions will tell a much more impressive story about who you are and what your organization can offer.

Walking out of any individual sales call, you should be able to gauge the value of investing any more time in the effort against the value of investing that same time somewhere else.

Redefining the salesperson

Dwight Schrute, salesman for fictional Dunder Mifflin paper company on *The Office,* says:

> Would I ever leave this company? Look, I'm all about loyalty. In fact, I feel like part of what I'm being paid for here is my loyalty. But if there were somewhere else that valued loyalty more highly, I'm going wherever they value loyalty the most.

Not everyone can pull off a solution-focused approach to sales calls. It requires people of substance and integrity who also possess these attributes:

- Honesty
- Expertise
- Self-confidence
- Charisma

Honesty

Ask the people who have to deliver what is sold if they would prefer a salesperson who wins big projects that cannot be executed or one who sells less, but puts the organization in a position to succeed.

Stereotypically slick sales patter does not solve problems and it cannot foster the healthy relationships that lead to successful, repeat engagements. Being direct, acting transparently, and speaking truthfully—even when the truth is uncomfortable—builds essential trust, respect, and confidence.

Tom Willis, the vice president of a property management firm that provides services to community associations in the Washington, D.C., area, says:

> **Set a pattern of little white lies and things like that and your brain gets rewired. You're building a habit. You're not going to be successful in the long run because you're going to lie to yourself and you're going to lie to other people.**
>
> **If you're in the service business, it's just a matter of time: You're not going to have quality relationships and you're not going to be successful in the long run.**
>
> **Honesty is everything, because as soon as you lose the confidence of your client, you're done.**

Honesty from the first sales call onward establishes a positive pattern of behavior. It raises client expectations, and those higher standards can lead to more and better opportunities.

Expertise

Rather than hiring salespeople and teaching them about engineering, some high-tech firms train engineers how to sell. It is recognition of a couple of factors: Technology can be overwhelmingly complicated and technology buyers can be surprisingly well informed. For those firms, it would be more dangerous to toss a sales professional in a room with the client's engineers than to send out an engineer who may have less polished sales skills. As a result, the sales-trained engineer can start grappling with clients' specific problems from the very first sales call.

Tom Willis listens for the moment during a sales call when the client stops talking to him like a salesperson:

> **Somehow or another, I've identified the thing or things that they've got issues with and I've started to create answers. I've started to create solutions for them.**
>
> **So they're not looking at me as someone trying to sell something artificial, they're looking at me as a resource for getting them where they want to go. And as soon as you flip that switch, you're there.**

A solution-focused sales call requires you to have expertise that is directly relevant to the client's challenges. If content strategy is at the heart of the project, for example, it may not be enough to have a salesperson who can speak to content strategy, but has never actually done that kind of work.

Self-confidence

Confidence in your ability to make a sale is nice to have; confidence in your ability to solve problems is essential. It frequently requires nimble translation of previous experiences to the conversation at hand. Self-confidence without real experience to justify it is weak, so identifying key tactics and applying them quickly is important.

No matter what kind of problem is at the foundation of a sales call, you should already have experience with:

- Defining complex problems (especially when details have been ambiguous)
- Recognizing relevant data from larger sets of data
- Identifying solutions (especially when they have been less than obvious to others)

Charisma

You would think that making a sale requires charisma, so what are you to do if that is not one of your strengths? You can fake charisma with some body language, strong eye contact, and a confident tone of voice, but sales calls need to stay honest.

It turns out, when you shift the sales call away from performance and toward problem solving, you can get away with quite a bit less charisma, so you might get by with whatever you have already got. You just might need to look for it to manifest itself in less obvious ways.

It would be a stretch to call Microsoft cofounder Bill Gates charismatic, but his intelligence and self-confidence make him hard to ignore. Film director Tim Burton's creativity and quirkiness overcome his radiating geek vibes. And say what you will about Hillary Clinton's lack of sizzle, she has been elected to the U.S. Senate, run as a Democratic presidential candidate, and served as the U.S. Secretary of State.

Some level of charisma is essential to motivate potential clients, as Tom Willis explains:

> **An effective leader recognizes the difference between motivation and manipulation and never ever crosses that line. In sales, it's the same thing.**
>
> **People assume they're being manipulated. They ask questions to make sure they're not being manipulated. You can tell by the tone of the conversation when that barrier has been broken: You've given them good information and there's a little level of excitement in the discussion. You've motivated them, but you haven't manipulated them. They believe that you're giving them quality things and they feel motivated by that.**

You need to figure out what flavor of charisma is already inside of you that will help clients feel motivated.

Meet the Expert: Nathan Brewer

As a vice president for global consulting firm Sapient, Nathan Brewer is heavily involved in the development of new client relationships.

•

Lower your emotional stakes

If you've done your homework and you're going in just to know the person, it lowers the stakes for you emotionally. You're thinking, "I just learned a whole lot about this interesting organization and I have 30 questions that I'd love to explore. I'm going in to have a conversation and it may or may not turn into something."

It takes that pressure off you so you get that chance to be genuine. You're just going in to learn and you're not stressing out thinking, "We gotta convert this, we gotta convert this."

Treat a sales call like a first date

The worst thing you could do on a first date is lead with: "I'm going to talk about myself for 45 minutes." You're never going to get a second date.

Yet when we go to these organizations, we think if we go in and talk about ourselves for 45 minutes that we'll actually get to the next step and build some sort of relationship.

Be genuine

One thing that's big in the sales press: "If you're in someone's office and you notice there's a soccer ball on the desk, then feign an interest in soccer."

You'll see a lot of professional salespeople do this and I think it's a complete amateur move. People sense genuineness and they know when you're BS-ing them.

Be a student

You may come away without solving anything, but that shouldn't be your desired outcome anyway. It should be getting to know them, building that relationship and, if something comes of it, fantastic. If something doesn't, you hopefully learned about a business or organization that you had no information about before.

Don't get too personal

People get freaked out if you've done too much personal research and you come in and say, "Oh, I saw that you went to Georgetown for undergrad and then you ...."

That freaks people out. That would freak me out if someone came in and did it to me.

What people buy

Sales calls are important, but they're unlikely to be the key to your organization's success. Your best customers come when someone they trusted hired you and then said good things about your work. Assuming you solve your clients' problems, work leads to more work. Referrals are a nice side effect of delivering exceptional value.

"Years ago, I would get all worked up if we made the effort and then didn't get the deal," says Tom Willis. "And now I don't care, because the bottom line is, even if we don't get the business then, we might get it two years from then or four years from then."

While your bills still have to be paid every month, success in selling services should always be considered over the long haul. The relationships you form with a client can play out over multiple projects and multiple years. It can all start with a single sales call where you focus on solving your potential client's problems instead of relying on sizzle reels and slick salesmanship.

Chapter 14

Mentoring

Mentoring is karma—offering a friendly ear or a guiding hand to honor all of the people who did the same for you once, or who will someday. It's helping people find their way—up, sideways, even out.

— Mark Stencel

Mentoring can be a vital part of personal and professional growth, both for the mentor and the people she guides. As your career progresses, it is likely that you'll have many opportunities to mentor and to be mentored. A mentoring relationship exists whenever someone with more experience in a specific area or field provides wisdom to one with less. Philosopher Socrates mentored Plato, poet Ralph Waldo Emerson mentored Henry David Thoreau, Jedi Obi-Wan Kenobi mentored Luke Skywalker.

Mentoring is really just a series of conversations, but we almost never let it stay that simple. We pore over mentoring books, videos, and websites. We attend (or create) mentoring seminars and conferences. We structure, sterilize, and standardize. The problem with all of these reasonable, orderly approaches is that they get applied to human beings and human beings are anything but reasonable and orderly.

Mentoring relationships get messy. Many of them evolve based on deeply personal, frequently emotional interactions. So if we want to study practical examples of mentoring, academic articles in the *Harvard Business Review* might not be the best source. Instead, we might want to turn to someone who has spent a career analyzing intense, emotional relationships: filmmaker Martin Scorsese.

Three types of mentoring

Scorsese has been making movies since the 1960s. He has earned a reputation for exploring brutal subjects, but even his bloodiest films tackle significant existential issues. He is a master at describing demanding relationships between complex characters and his depictions of mentorships are more riveting, and more relevant, than anything Harvard has come up with.

Scorsese's films provide an informative perspective on each of the three major types of mentoring: *Peer, career,* and *life.*

Peer mentoring in Goodfellas (1990)

Peer mentoring typically pairs entry-level coworkers so they can help each other get up to speed on how things are done within the organization. They work together to sharpen specific skills and learn basic professional practices.

In *Goodfellas*, Henry Hill (Ray Liotta) and Tommy DeVito (Joe Pesci) join the Mob as young men, both working for the neighborhood *capo*. In this scene, Tommy gives Henry a practical lesson in how one asserts power among peers within their organization.

> You mean, let me understand this because, you know maybe it's me, I'm a little f---ed up maybe, but I'm funny how? I mean funny like I'm a clown? I amuse you? I make you laugh, I'm here to f---ing amuse you? What do you mean funny? Funny how? How am I funny?

Although there are organizations that support peer mentoring programs, it most often happens unofficially and goes unrecognized as a mentoring situation even by the peers themselves. Peer mentorships can blossom into career-long relationships, but when they do they tend to evolve away from mentoring. Peer mentors are at their most valuable in the early stages of jobs or careers.

Career mentoring in The Color of Money (1986)

Career mentoring helps a professional who has attained some level of expertise gain additional skills. A seasoned mentor suggests ways to optimize the contributions of the less experienced professional in order to address the needs of the organization. The veteran can serve as an advisor and an advocate.

In *The Color of Money*, Fast Eddie Felson (Paul Newman) has not touched a cue in more than twenty years, but he knows more about poolhall hustling than Vincent Lauria (Tom Cruise) could ever imagine. In this scene, Felson intertwines subject matter expertise and flattery to deliver a withering assessment of Vincent's current career trajectory.

> **Eddie:** You're some piece of work. You're also a natural character.
>
> **Vincent:** You see? I been tellin' her that. I got natural character.
>
> **Eddie:** That's not what I said, kid. I said you *are* a natural character; you're an incredible flake. But that's a gift. Some guys spend half their lives trying to invent something like that. You walk into a poolroom with that go-go-go, the guys'll be killing each other trying to get to you. You got that. But I'll tell you something, kiddo: You couldn't find Big Time if you had a road map.

When people refer to mentoring, they're usually talking about career mentoring. This is the type of mentoring that organizations most often support and invest in. The roles of mentor and mentee are at their least ambiguous in career mentoring.

Life mentoring in The Departed (2006)

Life mentoring typically comes into play as people reach the middle of their careers and life mentors complement, rather than supplant, other mentors. While career-mentor conversations usually occur on a consistent basis, conversations with a life mentor happen only sporadically and tend to help address major challenges and decisions as they come up. A life mentor is expected to share hard-fought wisdom rather than regularly providing advice.

In *The Departed*, crime boss Frank Costello (Jack Nicholson) offers Colin Sullivan (Matt Damon) the benefit of his lifetime experience:

> **Frank:** When you decide to be something, you can be it. That's what they don't tell you in the church. When I was your age they would say we can become cops or criminals. Today, what I'm saying to you is this: When you're facing a loaded gun, what's the difference?

Life mentors can come from inside or outside the organization and can even work in different fields than those they advise. Life mentorships take time to initiate, but once engaged, life mentors tend to stay connected indefinitely with the people they help.

Mentoring variations

Technological advances and the introduction of social media tools have spawned variations on mentoring models.[1] Although none of these experimental forms have yet risen to the significance of peer, career, or life mentoring, they provide unique support at some organizations.

Anonymous mentoring

Psychological testing and a background review match employees with trained mentors (usually professional coaches or seasoned executives) outside the organization. Exchanges are conducted entirely online, and all parties remain anonymous. The engagement, generally paid for by the mentee's company, lasts six to twelve months.

Group mentoring

A self-organizing approach built for speed. One mentor works with several people at once. Face-to-face meetings, conference calls, and webcasts supplement online coaching. Two examples:

- AT&T: Mentoring takes place online in topic-based "leadership circles." The circles utilize community forums, document-sharing spaces, group polling, and calendars that announce events and mentor availability.

- BT (the British telecommunications firm): A peer-to-peer learning program built on a social collaboration platform that allows employees to pass on their knowledge and insights to their colleagues through five- and ten-minute audio and video podcasts, RSS feeds, and discussion threads.

Micro mentoring

Designed for younger employees accustomed to Twitter and text messaging, this peer mentoring approach uses quarterly reviews and an online, on-demand assessment system that limits feedback from other employees to 140 characters. The length limit forces people to think carefully about what they write, and because they must respond so immediately, they're able to provide highly relevant details. The software also collates the responses into a performance dashboard, so employees can track their own private trend lines on skills they are working to improve.

1   "Mentoring Millennials," *Harvard Business Review*, retrieved 9/9/12, http://hbr.org/2010/05/mentoring-millennials/ar/3

What kind of mentor are you?

This chapter is most relevant to career mentoring, although much of the information can also be useful for any type of mentoring. As mentioned earlier, most of us participate in peer mentoring without even recognizing it, so specific guidance on what it takes to be a good mentor and how to structure mentoring conversations may seem less applicable.

Like many of the "organizations" in Martin Scorsese's movies, you could find that once you get involved in mentoring, you'll be in it for life, eventually filling various roles in all forms of mentoring.

What it takes to be a good mentor

More than anything else, you need a good partner to be a good mentor. A healthy mentor relationship is an intersection of needs and value (**Figure 14.1**). Mentors fill the gap between what they know and what those being mentored need to know. Those on the receiving end are responsible for their own motivation. As Kim Bieler, a user-experience manager for information security company Mandiant, says:

> I like helping people who want to help themselves (as opposed to people who are just needy). When someone is motivated to be in a mentoring relationship, usually they already know what they want, they just need outside validation from someone who appears to be more experienced.

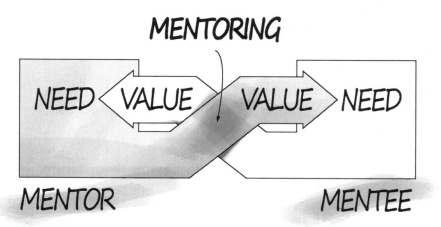

FIGURE 14.1 A four-way intersection of needs and value.

The more energy and determination the person being mentored brings to the relationship, the more likely it will be a true partnership that benefits both parties. Intel cofounder Andy Grove participated in a mentoring program that teamed technical assistants (TA) with senior executives:[2]

> **I had good experiences with my TAs because I would look for people who could teach me about some element I needed. In the 1980s I had a marketing manager named Dennis Carter. I probably learned more from him than anyone in my career.**

Both participants in a mentoring relationship are forced to explain themselves, to question what they think they know, and to defend their opinions. In defining their views for others, mentors get the opportunity to hear themselves talk about their own motivations.

Working through other people's issues forces mentors to reexamine their own experiences, or as Bieler explains it: "You have to work out your own shit before you can help someone else with the same problem."

In addition to a mutually beneficial relationship, successful mentoring also requires:

- Dancing skills

- A tactical mind

- Honesty

- An opinion

- A network

Dancing skills

Mentoring is like ballroom dancing and the mentor is expected to lead. In dancing, the lead must channel the combined energy of the couple in order to gracefully move across the floor without upsetting the other's balance.

The mentor takes a similar responsibility, skillfully directing the conversation's momentum while focusing on the needs of the mentee. A mentor has to follow the rhythm of every interaction, reacting more than acting, while being as elegant and coordinated as possible.

In both ballroom dancing and mentoring, flexibility is essential. As Priyanka Kakar, a manager of information architecture at Disney, points out:

> **The biggest responsibility is not pushing your mentee to do something that may not be right for them, but is comfortable for you, and continuing to stay a trusted advisor for them even if their values or needs don't align with yours.**

2 "Andy Grove: How to Be a Mentor," *BloombergBusinessweek*, retrieved 10/17/12, http://www.businessweek.com/magazine/andy-grove-how-to-be-a-mentor-09222011.html

Not all effective managers have the flexibility to be effective mentors. One reason for this is that a manager is expected to set direction, but a mentor must be more concerned with adjusting to the direction other people set for themselves.

An empathetic mentor keeps conversations anchored to the mentee's perspective. They listen more than they talk and they strive to hear information without filtering and without imposing their own judgments on what is said.

A tactical mind

While mentoring conversations should feel relaxed and informal, if they don't result in specific action for the mentee to take, they have little real value. A good mentor can convert the data of the conversation into relevant, meaningful tactics.

"The main thing I try to do when mentoring someone is help them take both short- and long-term approaches to the challenges they face," says David Panarelli, a user experience manager at LivingSocial.

Every mentoring conversation should advance the mentee in some way. When the mentor helps craft tangible outcomes, it makes that progress stick.

Honesty

Although most mentor relationships are friendly, not all are friendships. Direct, unflinching honesty can be difficult to maintain in a friendship, but is an essential requirement for mentoring.

"Honesty can be delivered gently or bluntly," says Mark Stencel, NPR's managing editor for digital news. "People who hear it seem to hear it the same way, no matter how gently or bluntly it's delivered. People who don't hear it just won't, even if you deliver it atop an intercontinental ballistic missile."

Honest, constructive criticism is expected of mentors, but it needs to be done with great care. Mentors should challenge their mentees without crushing their enthusiasm.

An opinion

While active listening is a foundation of effective mentoring, at some point mentors need to clearly articulate their opinions. It is through opinion that the mentee gets the benefit of the mentor's experiences and the wisdom earned during those experiences.

Every mentor has a unique way of dealing with what is one of the more subtle aspects of facilitating mentoring conversations. If she pushes too hard, she risks alienating or subjugating the other person; if she acts sheepishly, she has a better chance of obscuring value than exposing it.

It is the mentor's role to regularly challenge the mentee, but the mentor also has to know when to back down. Adam Polansky, a user experience strategist for Bottle Rocket, suggests:

> **When you have differing opinions with someone you mentor, have the discipline to recognize whether your opinion is truly better (and why) or just different. Let 'different' go.**

The goal should never be winning the argument. Mentors cannot allow themselves to compete with their partners, no matter how confident they are in their own opinion.

A network

A mentor is frequently part of a network of support that a talented mentee builds over the course of her career. A good mentor works in conjunction with past and present mentors and sets up the success of mentors to come.

Mentors vary in type (peer, career, life), experience (both in skills and depth), and relationship (coming from inside and outside the mentee's department or organization).

Mentors groom their charges to mentor others. User experience consultant Benno Schmidt suggests:

> **If you do your job really, really well when you are mentoring people, you will know that they will be taking care of the next guy, and the next guy, and the next guy. If you don't do your job well, then all those next guys are out of luck.**

How to design successful mentoring conversations

Mentoring is fragile stuff. A mentoring relationship is only as strong as the interaction of the two people at its core, so it's not surprising that larger programs and their inherent bureaucracies tend to weaken mentoring.

"Corporate mentoring programs are a charade. The intent behind them is good, but like everything the professionals get a hold of, they turn it into an incredibly complex and counterproductive routine," says Intel's Andy Grove.

The best mentor relationships transcend any corporate interference. If the organization's programs or policies hinder valuable interaction, it is the mentor's job to break the rules.

If necessary, you should take responsibility for structure. A solid structure, both across mentoring interactions and within a single interaction, can be a powerful tool in the protection and support of the mentoring relationship.

Structure includes:

- Frequency
- Agendas
- Ground rules

Frequency

Peer mentoring tends to happen on a daily basis, while a career mentor might schedule meetings a handful of times a year. With its emphasis on supporting major decisions, life mentoring tends to occur sporadically.

Even when regular meetings are working well, there can still be a need for unscheduled conversations. People should feel like they can connect with their mentors whenever it becomes necessary.

"I need to make myself available to them when they need help, not just when my schedule is open," says Viget CEO Brian Williams.

Agendas

Having an agenda for a mentoring conversation can help when participant expectations are misaligned. It also seems to comfort people who need the details of their lives hyperorganized.

An agenda should outline the key tasks that will be repeated for each conversation. For example:

1. Review major accomplishments since last meeting.

2. Discuss the mentee's current issues.

3. Discuss topics recommended by the mentor.

4. Formulate one to three action items to be accomplished before the next meeting.

Some mentors avoid agendas. Dan Brown, a principal of the consulting firm Eight-Shapes, prefers a subtler structure:

> Unlike other meetings, I generally don't set an agenda and let the person tell me a story about something that happened since the last discussion. Establishing this rhythm generally means that the person will start to keep an eye out for interesting challenges he or she would like to discuss.

Ground rules

Ground rules can be important when a mentoring relationship occurs between relative strangers or when the mentoring is highly visible in a politicized environment.

"It's risky to convey that you're picking and playing favorites," Mark Stencel explains. "Misunderstandings can create disappointment for the mentee or resentment for everyone else who's aware of the relationship."

Ground rules can be used to explicitly define:

- Boundaries: Appropriate catalysts for (and the timing of) mentoring conversations, appropriate work situations for discussion, and so on

- Expectations: Career goals, definitions of success, time required, and so on

- Discussion topics: Skill development, conflict resolution, and so on

Supporting mentees

Once a dependable structure is put in place by an organization or built by you, the focus can shift to providing support within each mentoring conversation.

In every conversation, offer a mix of:

- Guidance: Be humble, realistic, and specific about where you provide real value.

- Coaching: Maintain a qualified (rather than reckless) enthusiasm.

- Motivation: Pick the right times to kick them in the ass or pat them on the shoulder.

- Direction: Offer direction, but remember it's their decision whether or not to follow it.

- Constructive criticism: Criticize only what you can help correct.

Mentors can provide an additional service, which is often overlooked, in making the people they help feel smart. It just feels good to feel smart. We tend not to communicate the simple message that we value the intelligence of the people we work with. It can be significant when a mentor makes a point of explicitly talking about that respect. Polansky suggests:

> **Get their assessment of a situation and ask how they'd approach a problem before offering a solution. If you do offer solutions, ask if what you propose makes sense to them. If you have to criticize, never do it in public. Find what they do better than anyone else (including yourself). Distinguish that and make sure they know it.**

Adding unqualified support to the conversation doesn't require much additional effort, but the combination of both qualified and unqualified support can be surprisingly powerful.

Taking action

Whenever possible, mentoring conversations should result in clearly defined activities required of at least the mentee, if not both participants.

"I try to end with clear action items, otherwise it's just a nice little chat," says Panarelli.

Long-term action items are mentoring's equivalent of Twinkies: great in concept, but squishy and unsatisfying in actual execution. Overreaching items like "Optimize effectiveness across the organization within the next year" tend to devolve into wordsmithing exercises and result in little or no real progress.

Action items with quick turnarounds are the most effective. They should require people to convert conversational concepts into practical realities. Midterm action items can be useful in moderation. They may be necessary when challenges are too complex to complete quickly.

The value of mentoring

It's not hard to see the value of mentoring for those receiving it. Peer mentoring eases them into an organization and provides standards for conduct and execution. Career mentoring helps them optimize their expertise and strategize how to gain additional skills. Life mentoring exposes them to the wisdom of others when they need to make major decisions throughout their careers.

Mentoring does more for organizations than supporting the growth of individuals. Smart companies leverage mentoring every way they can. Williams, for example, treats it as a recruiting tactic at his company:

> Mentoring others effectively is essential to my business. Without good mentoring throughout our company, we'd never be able to attract and retain top talent.

Finally, mentoring brings significant value to the mentor. It helps her understand her own skills and expertise, reexamine her motivations, and analyze the key moments of her career.

One-on-Many Facilitation

There are times when you are center stage–be that in the center of an actual stage or just the single point of focus for a group of people who are interested in the content you are providing. You have the control of the content, and an audience who (in theory) is listening intently, providing only limited reactions and contributions. When you understand how to handle these scenarios, your confidence will shine through and make your content the star that it deserves to be front and center on the stage.

Chapter 15

Conference Presentations

According to most studies, people's number one fear is public speaking. Number two is death. Death is number two. Does that sound right? This means to the average person, if you go to a funeral, you're better off in the casket than doing the eulogy.

— Jerry Seinfeld

Mike: Listen, do you mind if I offer you a suggestion?

Jan: Oh, I'll take any advice I can get, Dad!

Mike: There's a famous old story about a man who had to get up and speak in front of some very important people–and he was petrified.

Jan: I'm with him!

Mike: Yeah. A friend gave him some advice: "When you get in front of those VIPs, you picture them sitting there in their underwear."

Jan: In their underwear?!

{everyone laughs}

Carol: Mike, is that true?

Mike: Sure it is! And it worked like a charm, too, because it made him real-ize that his audience was only human. I mean, you can't be very frightening in your underwear.

Alice: Well, you should see me in mine!

This scene from the 1970s series *The Brady Bunch* hits on a sensitive topic for a lot of people. Public speaking, it seems, is something that makes people quite nervous. And apparently imagining that you're standing in a roomful of half-naked people who are all staring at you is supposed to alleviate this fear.

The bad news is that if this is your fear, you are in the midst of a book that is pretty much making you stare it in the face. That can be pretty disconcerting, but tackling your fears head-on is one of the best ways to overcome them.

The good news is that most of the effort in public speaking is in the planning and preparation. We've endeavored to arm you with enough knowledge to get those plan-ning and preparation details out of the way so you can get up and do your thing.

The aspects of facilitation that most people align to public speaking are those that focus on presentations and panels. These are the times when you're putting all the focus in the room on you. You're putting your ideas out to the world to be judged and critiqued and, frankly, it's quite daunting.

Even if you're armed with the knowledge you need to be successful in a presenta-tion or on a panel, there are some other aspects that can help you keep your focus on your job as a presenter. The more you can do to remove distractions, the more your content will shine through.

Oh, and one other thing: The audience wants you to succeed. They showed up because of you and the content you've prepared for them. By the time you start presenting, you already have a room full of people who are rooting for you and who want to learn from you.

Can you think of a better position to start from?

Entrance: Stage right

All your preparation and planning helps to ensure that you have the information you need to speak to your audience intelligently. Extras such as slideshows, audio, and video can add to your content, but they shouldn't be the centerpiece of your presentation.

Any great presentation can be done in the absence of extras. But great presentations can't be accomplished without an audience and a location, both of which have their own benefits or challenges.

Presentation pregame

Somers White says:

> 90 percent of how well the talk will go is determined before the speaker steps on the platform.

The more you present, the more likely you are to find rituals that help you get into the right mindset and put you at ease. Christopher Fahey, UX lead at ZocDoc, suggests, "You aren't going to sleep the night before, so get plenty of sleep during the week leading up to the night before [you give a talk]." Final preparation of your material can be stressful. You may find yourself scrambling to finesse last-minute details—in some cases right up until it's time to present—so you may as well save some energy for that last big push by making sure you're well-rested along the way.

As Mark Twain put it:

> There are only two types of speakers in the world. 1. The nervous and 2. Liars.

Nerves will likely be a part of any presentation scenario you find yourself in. Consider how your body responds in stressful scenarios and plan accordingly. As Jesse James Garrett, cofounder and chief creative officer of Adaptive Path, recommends, "Have something small to eat, not a full [meal] or anything heavy. If you're going to have coffee [or caffeine], do it well before you have to be on stage." You won't need extra help in being nervous, and a heavy meal or extra energy can give your stomach a case of flip-flops on top of butterflies; it's far better to be a little hungry than a lot sick.

Marc Rettig points out a distinction between being nervous and being excited. It can be pretty easy to confuse the two feelings, and it's very important to recognize the difference!

Meet the Expert: Marc Rettig

Marc Rettig is the founding principal of Fit Associates, LLC, where he helps organizations grow healthy creative cultures that do work worth doing. He's been designing, researching, teaching, speaking, and facilitating for over 30 years, making him a professional at unfamiliar situations.

•

I still get nervous, but at someone's suggestion I'm learning to distinguish between scared and excited. They can feel similar. And I think it's mostly true that just before a talk I am more excited than afraid. At least that's true when I'm about to say something I really care about and believe in, even if it might be an act of courage to say it. If what I'm about to say doesn't excite me, then I have no business on stage.

Another lesson comes from David Whyte, my favorite poet-with-a-consulting-practice. He reminds us that the scared part of yourself really is part of you. Maybe it's the 13-year-old you. The thing is not to tell it to shut up, or man up, or stop being scared. The thing is to invite it on stage along with the confident part. He doesn't have to say anything, but you need him up there so it's *all* of you talking. The audience can read genuineness and vulnerability. It smells nothing like bullshit. They may or may not buy what you're saying, but they'll know you mean it.

It's OK to be nervous, excited, or both at the same time. These feelings are quite natural, and should be treated as reminders of why you're there. Feel free to acknowledge the existence of these feelings, and then grab them by the scruff and take them right to the stage with you. Be yourself and be invested in all the knowledge you have spent time planning and preparing and it will show.

And don't forget about biology! Alex Dittmer, an actor and musician, shares one of the habits he's learned over the years, "I always go pee when they call 'five minutes to places'—I'm not sure how I started the habit, but it seems to relax me." If you've ever seen a young child trying to "hold it in," then you know how it can look when you find yourself with too much time left to present and not enough time to, well, you know, make it.

Remember, these pregaming rituals can be different for different people. C. E. Lane, a professional musician, shares one of his self-observations over time, "It seems like there's some sort of inverse formula stating that the harder you are about to rock, the more silent you will become beforehand. Before the biggest show I ever played, I fell asleep under a card table." Your responses and reactions to presenting are unique to you, but not unique to the world at large. Rest assured that any crazy little quirks you uncover about yourself are probably shared with someone else.

Know the room

Every room is different, from the way the speakers and the audience are arranged to the way sounds bounce around them. These may seem like subtle details until you find yourself in a room that holds up to 2,000 people and only has about 100 spread throughout, and you have to figure out how to get your content to all of them in a meaningful manner.

(Pro tip: One crafty presenter at the WebVisions conference resolved this scenario by purchasing a few dozen Voodoo Doughnuts from the famous donut shop of that name in Portland, Oregon, placing them at the front of the stage, and offering them for free to anyone who was willing to come sit up front. Simple, brilliant, and worth the cost of the donuts to have an audience you can connect with.)

The room you're presenting in can impact the way you present. The amount of room you have to move around in, the placement of projector screens, the placement of your laptop—all of these can vary. Allow yourself enough time to "case the joint," or at least ask your host for photos of the room and its layout prior to arriving. You don't want to walk into a room expecting a round table that's suitable for activities only to find that you have rows of chairs and no space to collaborate and work in.

Find the room when it is empty and walk the space completely. Clap your hands and listen to how the sound reverberates in the room—take that into consideration as you're presenting. Have a friend listen to you speak from the stage or podium and tell you what the sound is like. Even if you'll be using a microphone, technology can fail and you should be prepared to go commando if you need to.

If you have the time and the opportunity, watch another presenter in your room and note any challenges that arise. Take as much time as you need to get comfortable in the space; it will be a space that you'll take ownership of and you want to leave little room for surprises.

Arrive at least an hour before your presentation to give yourself time to get settled in and set up, so when it's your turn you can focus on presenting. Take time to get to know your early arrivals and find people you can easily connect with during your talk. Many presenters find their "support" from the audience and will lock in on specific people who present them with feedback; finding those people early can help you keep your confidence level high.

Once you have your equipment set up, give it one last test to make sure everything is functioning properly. Maybe just one more time after that, too. Is your computer powered up and functioning? Do your slides project correctly or do you need to calibrate the display? Does your remote control work? Is the microphone picking up your voice? Do you have water for your presentation? Are you in the right room and at the right time? (Find more details on managing your room layout in Chapter 5, "Environment.") These may seem like very obvious questions and, to some degree, problems that other people should deal with, but you should make sure that you are answering these so you can move forward with your Plan B.

Uh...you have a Plan B, right?

Presentation time

Michael H. Mescon tells us:

> **Best way to conquer stage fright is to know what you're talking about.**

This is the moment that all your long-term planning and last-minute checking under the hood have prepared you for. You're bound to be nervous and excited, and that shouldn't really be a surprise. You'll learn over time how to best manage and internalize those feelings. In the meantime, you really ought to get on with it.

Talking about yourself

In most cases, when you're presenting or on a panel of some sort, people have been invited to attend or have paid hard-earned money to be in the audience. This means that you and your topic, as well as a supporting description, were a big part of why they've decided to be there. Since you'll probably have limited time to spend on your topic, spend as much as you can speaking on that topic and hammering your key points home, and as little time as possible showcasing who you are and why you should be there. It's okay to work your background into your comments by saying something like, "When I was at Stuffed Shirt and A'holes, we did it this way...," so the audience has some details without you reading from your resume. People have already made up their minds about you and your content if they are in the audience; convince them with content and not with biographies and bragging.

Are there exceptions to this? Absolutely! There are plenty of cases where your background and information may be very relevant to what you're about to share. Don't be afraid to spend time describing your background and history when it's relevant and required. However, when the information has already been provided to the attendees prior to the presentation or panel, it's best to just get on with sharing your brilliance!

Someone may introduce you to the audience. In many cases, those kind folks who introduce you spend a lot less time researching and preparing for their subject than you do. This is okay; it takes some of the pressure off you and prevents you from spending more than the minimum amount of time talking about yourself! One of the best ways to make sure this happens smoothly is to bring a printed copy of your introduction with you. Keep it brief, but highlight any professional and personal items that you find relevant and worth sharing. Consider including a sentence or two about what you'll be speaking about so the transition to you can be more fluid and natural.

If you have been introduced, it makes for an easy transition to kicking off your presentation with some housekeeping and courtesies. Make sure you thank your hosts (if you have them), welcome your audience, acknowledge any previous presenters, and provide any rules of engagement during the presentation. If you have not been formally introduced to the audience and it adds value to your presentation, briefly share your background and qualifications.

Stage presence

Stage presence is a big part of getting your message to your audience. Do your best to minimize your own distracting actions and behaviors—many of which you may find out about after you have the opportunity to watch yourself present on video, which is daunting and often cringe-worthy on its own! You can, however, practice good posture, make eye contact with people you see or meet, pay attention to your hands as you're speaking, and control the volume of your voice, your tone, and your enunciation as you talk to different people in different scenarios. Pay close attention to your habits—good and bad—as you engage with others and make mental notes and adjustments as you go.

Timothy J. Koegel, author of *The Exceptional Presenter* (Greenleaf Book Group Press, 2007) recommends five tips for a good stage presence:

1. Stand tall.

2. Keep your head and eyes up.

3. Smile.

4. Never retreat.

5. Move with purpose, energy, and enthusiasm.

In addition to showing your confidence and being engaging and enthusiastic about your topic, there are a few other tips to be aware of.

Eye contact is key. It's not always easy to do, but look around the room. Make connections with people, even if briefly. If you find it difficult or distracting, try looking about a foot above a row of foreheads; it gives the impression that you're looking at your audience without being above them. Don't breeze past the entire audience; pace yourself and take moments to pause.

Know where your microphone is and how to best use it. If you're using a lapel microphone, remember which side it's on and don't turn your head away from it while speaking. If you're using a handheld microphone, make sure you know how close or far away from your mouth it needs to be for the audience to hear you clearly.

OMG your hands! Beware of dinosaurs and other creatures. There are so many other things to focus on that it can be easy to lose track of what your hands are doing. Some people may not even be aware that they have a wildly flailing appendage that completely distracts from the rest of their presentation. Even worse, don't fall into the trap of the "T-Rex," as Koegel calls. To understand what this position looks like, lock your elbows to your ribs and pick up a coin, using only your thumb and index finger on each hand. Now, roar. Feels silly, doesn't it? Be mindful of the characters you may be imitating, and do your best to slay them before you get on stage.

Podiums are not hidey holes. This seems obvious, but it can be easy to use a podium as a crutch or separator between you and the audience. You can be behind the podium without having it impede your performance. Don't get lazy behind it; it's not there to support you, either physically or emotionally, so keep your hands off it as much as you can and keep your eyes on the audience. Make sure you're engaging the entire room, not just the people directly in front of the podium. There's an entire room full of people to be aware of.

Use your words. So...you know, like, your, umm...words. Nerves, excitement, and being completely in the moment during a presentation can make you oblivious to the differences between the words flying through your brain and the words shooting out of your mouth. If your noise-to-signal ratio is too high, you can undercut all the valuable information that you're sharing, so try to remember to...

Slow down and breathe. Presentation time is much different as the presenter than it is as the audience member. No matter how many times you rehearse, time moves differently when you're on stage and presenting, so make sure you follow up your great points with a good pause.

Again, Mark Twain:

> **The right word may be effective, but no word was ever as effective as a rightly timed pause.**

Your audience will need time to digest your brilliance, make a note of it, and most likely, share it with some other social media audience. Give them the time to do that, and provide the emphasis needed by giving the point a moment before moving on to the next one.

You have the voice and the authority. All eyes and ears are on you, and you have the power to make things happen. Politely shush your audience and they will give you the silence you request. Ask your audience for a show of hands in response to a question, and hands will fly up. Ask your audience to stand and take part in an activity, and they will move. This power is yours to command, but use it wisely and with control and purpose.

Caught in the act

Even the masters will tell you that, from time to time, something happens that will cause you to lose your train of thought, most likely when you're right in the middle of making a strong point. (Read some great examples in Chapter 20, "Horror Stories.") Singer, songwriter, and actor Eytan Mirsky reminds us, "Most times, people are not as aware of any mistakes as you might think. They are not focusing on things the way you, as the [presenter], are." It's easy to fall into the trap of panicking, but it's best if you can keep your cool, slow yourself down, and see if you can continue without going off the rails.

If all else fails, be honest with yourself and your audience. Erik Soens, speaker and professional musician, shares how he dusts himself off after losing his flow, "A simple statement such as, 'Whew... that got away from me; let me reiterate' works just fine."

Your audience will be forgiving; mistakes happen all the time and you want to provide them with the knowledge that they showed up to gain.

Reading the audience

Many presenters find that their audience provides them with the feedback and energy they need to be successful. When you can read the reactions of your audience, it helps you understand where you can spend time going deeper on some topics and cut short the explanations for other areas.

Audiences come in all shapes and sizes. You may present to an audience that is engaged and participating and turn around and present the same content to another audience that seems to be asleep at the wheel. You'll wonder what was different in the audience or what you did differently with the material, but there are many factors that could be out of your control.

Some common types of audience members you may encounter are:

Leaners and nodders. These people are your gravy train. Look for them early, and check in on them often. They're the ones who most want you to succeed and who are locked in to your content. They are your support in the moments when you feel your confidence waning.

People you know. These can be your friends—the ones who throw you a softball question to help you succeed, or who simply sit in a row closer to the front to provide support, or even those who may heckle you. They can also be coworkers, family members, or other acquaintances, and they can be a mixed blessing. Some of them are supporters, and some of them are intimidators, whether they know it or not.

Recorders. Some people attend presentations with the intention of recording all the content. These may be members of the press, those who are required to present their findings back to a team at their workplace, or even folks who are live-recording the event to social networks. These folks appear to not be paying attention to you, but they're likely to be heads-down capturing your every word. Sometimes you get lucky and one of your recorders is visually capturing your presentation in sketchnote format.

In this room, but doing something else. Believe it or not, some people will camp in the room where you're presenting only so they can have a place to work on something else. They may be sending emails or instant messages or handling other business that demands their attention more than you do. They might even be other presenters working on their own material. They are generally hiding out in remote corners where they don't draw much attention, and make it easy for you to disregard them while you're presenting.

Sleepers. This may happen even if you're rockin' like Dokken. Sorry, sometimes it's them and not you. But sometimes it's you, too.

Leavers. Sometimes, people leave. They may feel that the content you're delivering is not what they're looking for, or they may simply have to be somewhere else, such as the restroom or on a business call. Don't let leavers distract you; focus on the people in the room and deliver your content to them and for them.

Responders and contributors. These are your true participants; they're engaged and actively take part in whatever you ask of them. They interact with you and the rest of the audience in positive ways that help keep your energy and confidence levels high. Treat them with respect and cherish their attendance.

There are many types of audience members, and the makeup of your audience can impact the room just as much as your own stage presence can.

The peak-end rule

Psychologist and Nobel laureate Daniel Kahneman, author of *Well-Being: Foundations of Hedonic Psychology,* noted that people tend to create biased memories of an experience based "almost entirely on how they were at their peak (pleasant or unpleasant) and how they ended. Virtually all other information appears to be discarded, including net pleasantness or unpleasantness and how long the experience lasted" (Russell Sage Foundation Publications, 2003).

It should be easy to see how this should impact your presentations. If your audience will remember the highest peak of your presentation, as well as how you ended it, then you've established your targets. Aim for a really strong peak in your presentation, be it a cat video that supports a claim in a metaphorical fashion or a definition for UX that everyone can agree on universally. Challenge yourself to close on a highly energetic, positive note that meets the needs of your audience.

Panels

At first blush, panels appear to be simple to undertake. The reality is that there's a lot to consider when you're part of a panel, and even though most of the same presentation rules apply, the differences are worth noting.

A good panel size is generally four to five panelists, plus a moderator. Ideally, panelists have depth of expertise and experience on your topic, and more importantly, varying opinions.

As a panelist, you should be familiar with the topic or theme and have an opinion about it. If you find yourself being asked to be on a panel that you don't feel strongly about, evaluate whether or not it makes sense for you to remain on the panel; the attendees deserve the best information they can get from people who are passionate about the topic. If you've been given background information or preparatory questions, familiarize yourself with them, but don't use prepared, canned answers. Instead, think about related experience you can pull from and share more natural responses.

As a moderator, you have the toughest job. In addition to herding the rest of the panelists, the moderator needs to know the topic as well as enough about the panelists to keep the conversation flowing. The moderator should know how to keep the perspectives coming from the other panelists, but also when to politely cut off conversation that starts to spin away from the topic at hand. One last thing: The moderator should know that he or she is directing a panel of experts, and it's not the moderator's job to be the star, but instead, to make stars out of the panelists and their content.

Some panels may have slides or other materials that are prepared in advance. While this is OK, the panel may quickly devolve into a group presentation if the moderator is not imposing fairly strict restrictions on how much time may be spent on this type of content. Panelists often have a lot to say on their topic and part of the role of the moderator is to manage that. Good cop, bad cop—whichever; the moderator is definitely time cop.

Try to avoid sit-down-at-the-table-with-a-name-placard-in-front-of-you panels. These settings let panelists get a little lazy and make it easier to disconnect from what's happening. Avoid using computers or devices; these can easily prove distracting and the audience and other panelists will easily pick up on an unfocused member of the panel. Some of the best panels happen when the panelists sit in a way that lets them engage with the moderator, one another, and the audience. See if you can arrange a setup that provides a more open view of the panel—a little extra body language goes a long way with an audience.

Exit: Stage left

Once you've completed your presentation, it can be pretty easy to pack up your stuff and head for the door. If there's time remaining or time has been designated for questions and answers, you may choose to continue to engage your audience. (For additional information on this, see Chapter 18, "Managing Questions and Answers.") If you've used up the time designated for your presentation, be courteous to your audience and end on time—they may be allowed a break or they may need to move to their next presentation if there are multiple tracks at the event. Be mindful of the next presenter and tear down any of your equipment to make room for them to set up.

Take some time to appreciate your audience and thank them for their time. If not for the audience, your ability to share your knowledge would be dramatically reduced, or at least relegated to other venues. Make yourself available for follow-up questions and comments, and be sure you have plenty of business cards to share. If you're going to share your materials online, such as by posting your slides to Slide-Share (http://slideshare.net), let the attendees know if and when they're available.

It's important to remember that presentations generally happen because someone else invested a lot of time and energy in planning an event. This involves securing a date and time, locating a venue, marketing to an audience, and other details. Thank your hosts not only to your audience, but also to the hosts themselves. Proper event planning is challenging work, and a handwritten "thank you" note goes a long way toward showing your appreciation for being able to share what you've learned with others.

Chapter 16

Virtual Seminars

If there was a way to make virtual seminars more about interaction and less about getting presented to on a topic, then I think as a student and as a teacher, I would get more out of it.

— Samantha Starmer

You know that obnoxious guy who keeps showing up uninvited to your friends' parties? The one who always gets there too early so he can get sloppy drunk on the free booze and then spends the rest of the night talking about the other parties he has crashed? Technology is like that; it disrupts everything.

Modernized machinery made English textile artisans a quaint memory in the nineteenth century. Soon after, the internal combustion engine bankrupted horse-related industries. By the end of the twentieth century, technological advances triggered a disruption that rolled through the music industry as compact discs replaced long-playing records and then online distribution replaced CDs.

Technology has stumbled its way through a bunch of Internet-related parties over the last couple of decades and now it is pounding on education's front door. Some examples:

- Salman Khan, a hedge fund analyst, started posting instructional videos on YouTube in 2006 and now runs Khan Academy, whose online classes have been viewed more than 200 million times. Six million unique students use the site each month.[1] Volunteers have translated Khan's videos into 24 different languages, including Urdu, Swahili, and Chinese.

- Stanford University made a course called "Introduction to Artificial Intelligence" available on the Internet in 2011 and 160,000 people from 190 countries enrolled.[2]

- In May 2012, Harvard University and the Massachusetts Institute of Technology each committed $30 million in institutional support, grants, and philanthropy to launch a not-for-profit organization that offers online instructional content.[3]

Virtual seminars are online presentations delivered from anywhere and available to anyone with the right permission and an Internet connection, and they're disrupting traditional approaches to teaching lessons.

They're having an effect in less formal educational environments as well. User Interface Engineering (UIE), for example, has been selling virtual seminars since 2007. Instead of trudging from conference to conference, authors and other prominent speakers present their content once and UIE distributes their work to people all over the world.

With the potential for a much larger audience spread across the globe and irrespective of time (recorded seminars are made available after presentation), what is there for an ambitious speaker or educator not to love?

1   Michael Noer, "One Man, One Computer, 10 Million Students: How Kahn Academy is Reinventing Education," *Forbes*, November 19, 2012. Retrieved Dec. 10, 2012. http://www.forbes.com/sites/michaelnoer/2012/11/02/one-man-one-computer-10-million-students-how-khan-academy-is-reinventing-education/

2   Tamar Lewin, "Instruction for Masses Knocks Down Campus Walls," *The New York Times*, March 4, 2012. Retrieved Dec. 11, 2012. http://www.nytimes.com/2012/03/05/education/moocs-large-courses-open-to-all-topple-campus-walls.html

3   Source: Laura Pappano, "The Year of the MOOC," *The New York Times*, November 2, 2012. Retrieved Dec. 10, 2012. http://www.nytimes.com/2012/11/04/education/edlife/massive-open-online-courses-are-multiplying-at-a-rapid-pace.html

The trouble with virtual seminars

Virtual seminars have a dirty little secret: They force speakers to break just about every best practice for delivering quality presentations. Issues for most virtual seminars include:

- Speakers can't see their audience, let alone engage them.

- Presentations rely heavily on slides rather than speaker delivery.

- Support for audience interaction is limited and clumsy.

Dave Malouf, who taught several courses at the Savannah College of Art and Design, is uncomfortable using today's conferencing tools:

> **I don't think my teaching style works virtually. I'm not a very good talking head. I'm much better engaging people, asking people questions, using people as fodder for the material and the conversation. It's really hard to do that when the people aren't right in front of you.**

The tools available today just are not up to the challenges of the emerging opportunity.

Underdeveloped tools

Popular online conferencing tools like GoToMeeting, WebEx, and Adobe Connect focus on the wrong aspects of virtual seminars. Instead of trying to support the transfer of knowledge from the speaker to participants' brains, companies get distracted by the capabilities of a computer. Learning success comes when the tools aid the absorption, processing, and retention of information, but companies compete mainly on chat, screen sharing, and video functionality.

Text-based chat

Like many aspects of virtual seminars, the concept of chat is better than its reality. If a speaker is typing or reviewing text messages from participants, she cannot present at the same time. If a speaker wants to take advantage of chat tools, she has to outsource the most important aspect of traditional presentations: interaction with the audience.

Some speakers have tried to address this challenge by creating the role of moderator for the person who monitors the chat window during the presentation. But it's a rare tag team that can effectively pull off the synchronization between speaking and moderating.

Even in well-coordinated efforts, the best you can expect is that the moderator has skillfully timed the insertion of audience questions into the presentation. But that's weak support for the best parts of Q&A, when the speaker and an audience member work together to discover the real issue behind a question.

Chat tools have been developed for short, objective answers, while the more interesting questions tend to be the ones that defy simple responses.

Finally, the typical delay between when an audience member enters chat text and when that text actually appears on-screen means people would be better off Googling to find the answers to their questions.

Screen sharing

Virtual seminar presenters who depend on complex visual communication put themselves completely at the mercy of Internet service providers. Upload and download speeds fluctuate wildly during a typical presentation. This means that the speaker can never trust that what he sees on his screen is what the audience is experiencing. Trying anything more ambitious than static text slides, like animation or tricky transitions, can be foolish.

And what would the speaker actually want to share from his screen? Sure, there's an algebraic logic to it—presenting is sharing information, computer screens are full of information, therefore presenting should include sharing computer screens—but it doesn't hold up in practice. The key here is the presentation's *context of use.* People listen to music in their cars, but manufacturers don't build trumpets into steering wheels, because the primary experience of a car is driving, not making music. The primary experience of a presentation is the transfer of information, not sharing the tools that might have crafted that information.

Video

Video cameras are built into just about every new device. This is especially true for computers, tablets, and mobile phones. But when it comes to virtual seminars, video content is a brilliant solution still looking for a problem to solve.

When you present a virtual seminar, you're essentially playing in a room by yourself. That rarely makes good video. (There's an obvious exception to this, but live pornography is a kind of conversation that this book makes no attempt to help you design. You're on your own.)

When a speaker depends on slides, the audience gets the treat of watching someone talking and staring off to the side of the camera.

Lack of interaction

Hopefully, the direction of virtual seminar tool development will shift from computer capabilities to something more useful, like the interaction between speaker and audience. Kent State Assistant Professor Karl Fast says:

> **When you're lecturing in front of people face-to-face, you can tell when people are really confused about something, or they don't really get it. You need to respond to that.**

Future development will have to address three primary issues: energy, accountability, and the inevitable overreliance on slides.

Energy

There's a reason why editors are so respected in the film industry. A hundred years ago, filmmakers realized that they had to start moving their cameras around. That created piles of footage showing the same action from multiple camera angles. And that in turn created the need for people who could build tension by cutting together shifts in perspective.

As part of a live presentation, a good speaker uses body language and movement to communicate information and create emotional energy, not unlike a good theater actor. But as in early film, the fixed position of the cameras used for most virtual seminars kills any potential for energy.

Energy from a live speaker triggers the energy of the audience, creating a powerful cycle. Right now, that back-and-forth transfer is rare for a virtual seminar.

Also, with participants experiencing the seminar from a wide variety of locations, the speaker's disembodied voice can have a chilling effect on the energy of everybody involved. (Plus it's just plain creepy.)

Accountability

A live presentation or a lecture is a contract between the speaker and her audience. You, the audience, will invest your time. She, the presenter, will provide value that justifies that investment. The presenter of a virtual seminar makes the same commitment to deliver value, but the audience is not held accountable. They have logged in to the seminar perhaps, but it is nobody's business if they decide to watch television at the same time, or clean the toilet, or continue doing some other form of billable work.

Without the need to be present, the contract is broken and a certain level of intensity is lost.

Reliance on slides

The many underwhelming tools for virtual seminars leave a presenter with just one tool: her slides. Ironically, the highly visual, textually spartan decks that work so well in person leave the virtual seminar audience with little to look at.

But while giving them slides crammed with text would give them something to study, that cannot possibly be a good idea. It is a real quandary.

Solutions

In *Confessions of a Public Speaker*, Scott Berkun says:

> **Go to a place in your mind where you remember the last time you spoke to a live, friendly, interested group, and match that style of behavior and enthusiasm. Speak as if that same audience is listening, and you'll be fine.**

Some people can pull off Berkun's Method-acting approach for presenting without an audience. Those who can't should consider one of these three tactics:

- Stage a great radio drama.
- Be the UPS guy.
- Go TED.

These tactics can be implemented individually or combined, depending on the needs of the virtual seminar creator.

Stage a great radio drama

Radio dominated U.S. popular culture in the 1930s and 1940s with programs that included live drama, comedy, and music and featured the biggest names in entertainment. Trained in the live theater, some of those stars insisted on a studio audience for their programs.

While virtual seminars need only a speaker and the equipment to broadcast and record the lecture, bringing a small group of observers into the room can energize the presentation just as much as studio audiences did for Jack Benny or the cast of *Fibber McGee and Molly* nearly a century ago.

Why it works

A good speaker pays attention to the reactions of her audience. She speeds up or slows down her rhythm, makes tiny adjustments in emphasis, reviews content when the audience seems lost, and skips ahead when the audience gets bored. It turns out that when the seminar is experienced by a new, disaggregated audience, they tend to respond to the speaker's sensitivity in the same ways as the original audience. These refinements make for better presentations in both content and performance.

How to do it

Virtual seminar creators have it much easier than early radio producers, who had to rent theaters and deal with tickets and other complex organizational challenges. All it takes for online presentations is four to eight people, enough to fill the seats of a single conference table. They can be friends or strangers—the only requirement is that they find the subject of the seminar interesting.

Have the audience surround the speaker at the table. The speaker more than likely will want to perform sitting down so she won't stray too far from her equipment. The speaker should play to the audience in the room, reacting to their responses, feeding off their energy.

Be the UPS guy

Do you remember the United Parcel Service (UPS) commercial where a man with longish hair creates quick, informal sketches as he describes shipping services? The man, Andy Azula, a creative director for the advertising agency that produced the ads, ended up making 52 of the commercials. Each is a study in effective communication that intertwines verbal and visual information. Not everyone can so confidently draw and talk at the same time, but the technique is so powerful that it can be effective even when done much less elegantly than Azula did.

Without any formal presentation or instructional experience, Salman Khan used a similar approach to create about three thousand lessons for his Khan Academy. Khan's videos start with a blank digital blackboard, and over the 10-minute lesson he provides commentary as he fills up the screen with brightly colored illustrations that describe key concepts.

Why it works

In *Blah Blah Blah: What to Do When Words Don't Work*, Dan Roam says:

> **Making sure that our verbal and visual minds are working together is the simplest thing in the world. We say a word, we draw a picture. The two halves of our mind have been working together for millions of years and know exactly how to do it. We're just out of practice.**

The more visual the information, the more likely it is to be retained.[4] From an evolutionary perspective, our relatively recent fascination with written and verbal communication, often at the expense of the visual, is unnatural. Moving and thinking have always been part of a package deal for humans, with movement relying heavily on the management of visual data. Dwindling food supplies one hundred thousand years ago triggered constant migration and required endless adjustment to new environments with unknown predators. The same mechanisms that kept us from extinction then make us pay attention now when somebody starts drawing to explain a concept.

How to do it

Consider these steps for crafting a UPS guy presentation or lesson:

- Design or revise the structure so it's based on a series of concepts.

- Develop a single visual explanation for each concept. The words you use, whether you're in front of the camera like Azula or lurking behind illustrations like Khan, are still important, but they must always support the visual communication.

- Find a sketching tool that you're comfortable with, ideally one you've used in the past on the same computer you'll use for your virtual seminar.

- Practice building each illustration while speaking, to the point where you no longer need to refer to your notes. The purpose is not to improve the craftsmanship of the illustration. Illustrations have to be effective; it doesn't really matter if they're pretty.

- Repurpose the screen-sharing tool of your online conferencing software to support live drawing.

---

4   John Medina, *Brain Rules* (Seattle: Pear Press, 2008), 233.

Free drawing tools

Live sketching doesn't always require investing in a tablet and stylus or learning complex software. These sites offer free online drawing tools:

- www.kerpoof.com
- pencilmadness.com
- www.slimber.com
- www.wixie.com

Go TED

This approach is likely to scare away less experienced presenters. Instead of dealing with slides and creepy disembodied voices, consider going to the other extreme and making your presentation with no slides.

Almost thirty years ago, a group of organizers brought together people from the technology, entertainment, and design industries for a conference devoted to "ideas worth spreading." More conferences followed and now over 1,400 TED talks are available for viewing online. TED talks have set a high standard for presentations. Speakers have included scientists, rock stars, magicians, CEOs, and a former U.S. president. They're encouraged to dream big, strip away pretense, and make the complex simple. They perform alone, standing without a podium or a laptop. Slides are rare and even when they do appear, they are never more than supplemental to the talk.

Why it works

It really comes down to vulnerability. Without structures or artifacts to hide behind, the speaker is exposed to potential ridicule and embarrassment and that commitment is hard for even a virtual audience to ignore. Even though a speaker and an audience member may never meet, a powerful emotional bond can be formed.

Also, the confidence required to "go TED" plays well in the performance. The audience wants the speaker to do well and a confident demeanor can quickly create the perception of success.

How to do it

It is not necessary to meet a TED talk's highest standard. Public speaker and author Nancy Duarte recommends rehearsing an hour for each minute of a TED-style talk.[5] That may not be feasible for a virtual seminar, certainly for a lesson that is one of many for a course, but succeeding while standing alone and metaphorically naked will take as much practice as you can fit into your schedule.

Boil your notes down to their essence and put them on a slide deck. Display the slides for your own benefit, just below the camera you'll be speaking into. You would never read visible slides to your audience (a terrible sin), but using the hidden deck to keep track of your argument is essential. More tips:

- Present standing up with a dark or monotone background.

- Speak directly into the camera.

- Take advantage of a lavalier microphone if you have one. If you have to go with a handheld microphone, make sure you get plenty of time to practice using it.

- Movement in front of the camera is fine as long as it doesn't make you look antsy.

The future

This will sound contrary to most of what has been said in this chapter, but machines will eventually do a better job of delivering one-to-one virtual seminars than humans, especially in academic and training environments.

Individual lessons, intertwined with regular quiz-like assessments, will adapt according to the needs of each audience member. System development will be guided by the workings of the human brain rather than distracted by the limitations of computer hardware and software:

> **These systems [will] allow instructors to track students' progress through a course of study at a fine-grained level of detail, thereby enabling more targeted and effective guidance. Such systems are far beyond the capability of individual instructors to create on their own, and are typically developed by teams of cognitive scientists, software engineers, instructional designers, and user interface experts.**[6]

---

5 Nancy Duarte, "10 Ways to Prepare for a TED-format Talk," *Duarte.com*, February 28, 2011. Retrieved December 15, 2012. http://blog.duarte.com/2011/02/10-ways-to-prepare-for-a-ted-format-talk/

6 Lawrence S. Bacow, et al, "Barriers to Adoption of Online Learning Systems in U.S. Higher Education," ITHAKA S+R, May 2012. Retrieved Dec. 16, 2012. http://www.sr.ithaka.org/sites/default/files/reports/barriers-to-adoption-of-online-learning-systems-in-us-higher-education.pdf

Instead of evolving their way to a better solution, online conferencing tools may turn out to be transitional, serving a need only until a more appropriate solution emerges. The audio technology of vinyl records dominated its industry for 50 years, but the video technology of VHS tapes lasted less than half that time.

The current approach to virtual seminars may survive or it might be a bridge to something much better. In either case, it is likely that the technology behind the tools will continue to stumble around like a bad drunk at a party.

Technology is not the key to designing successful virtual seminars. Disruptive capabilities have emerged along with the Internet and it is the ability and willingness of speakers and educators to innovate in the face of that disruption that will determine success or failure.

Chapter 17

Lectures

There is no more agreement about what is a good lecture than there is about good music.
— Donald Bligh

Dave Malouf walked into the third class of his Contextual Research Methods course not knowing what the hell he was going to do and walked out two-and-a-half hours later with a new, radically different lecturing style.

Most of Malouf's presentation experience had been at industry conferences before coming to teach at the Savannah College of Art and Design in Georgia. At conferences, his peers expected highly polished slides, so when he started teaching, he assumed the same would be true in the classroom. He lectured accordingly.

He had been reworking the course's content that quarter and fell behind in rewriting his lectures. Staring at a roomful of undergrads without a viable deck, Malouf had no choice but to go commando, without slides:

> I just shot from the hip. It went better than lecturing with a perfect deck because all of a sudden I saw that everyone was taking notes and there were more questions being asked. From then on, I played with it, trying to find the right balance between being a hundred-percent-prepared formal versus from-the-hip-loose conversational.

It worked because Malouf had narrowed the gap between what he said and what students heard. Success in the classroom came not only from him finding a style closer to his true voice, but also by better aligning his lecture with the ways that human beings think and learn.

How we think

The process of thinking relies on four factors (**Figure 17.1**):[1]

- Information coming from the environment
- Information stored in long-term memory
- Procedures stored in long-term memory
- Space available in working memory

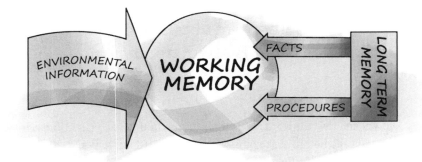

FIGURE 17.1 Thinking occurs in working memory.

Long-term memory is a warehouse where we store information we have acquired and procedures we have used in the past to execute tasks. It is a surprisingly large storage space, so large in fact that our minds are careful to never let us see the complete, overwhelming inventory. We are aware of things from long-term memory only when they are temporarily shipped out to our working memory, the part of the mind that keeps track of the environment around us.

---

1   Willingham, D. (Spring 2009). Why Don't Students Like School. *American Educator*, pp. 4-13.
http://www.aft.org/pdfs/americaneducator/spring2009/Willingham(2).pdf

Thinking takes place in working memory when information from the environment combines with a few facts and procedures on loan from long-term memory.

Imagine you are sitting in class and the lecturer spontaneously bursts into flames. Environmental details about the flames and the lecturer's reaction flood your working memory—as do the stored facts that fire harms flesh and that you previously saw an extinguisher in the hallway. Your mind quickly combines that information with other items from your long-term memory, including the procedures for exiting the classroom to retrieve the extinguisher and for operating it. That kind of quick thinking might get you an A in the class from a grateful, somewhat toasty instructor.

Tactics for how we think

In designing lectures, it is important to understand how humans think, because without proper planning, they may not. Daniel Willingham, cognitive psychologist, explains:[2]

> **The brain is not designed for thinking. It's designed to save you from having to think, because the brain is actually not very good at thinking... Your brain serves many purposes, and thinking is not the one it does best. Your brain also supports the ability to see and to move, for example, and these functions operate much more efficiently and reliably than our ability to think.**

If the brain can respond to a challenge solely with information from long-term memory, it almost always will. The first time you used a can opener, your mind probably considered the purpose of the opener's handle and the function of its gears. By the third or fourth use, your brain had actually changed so that thinking was not required to open the can. As much as possible, every lecture should be a fresh challenge that demands that students' brains function at a level higher.

In addition to transcending rote memorization, a lecturer should focus on her students' working memories, where space is always precious. The more room available for thinking, the more receptive students will be to a lecture.

Multistep instructions, unfamiliar terms, and ambiguity can quickly clog working memory, while clarity, regular reviews of information, and references to previously mastered concepts can create more room for thinking.

---

2   Willingham, D. (Spring 2009). Why Don't Students Like School. *American Educator*, pg. 4.
http://www.aft.org/pdfs/americaneducator/spring2009/Willingham(2).pdf

How we learn

The brain stores and recalls complex bundles of information all the time. It should be no surprise then that such an active machine does not suddenly become passive when it comes to learning. Yet for generations, educators treated students as empty vessels in need of filling.

The constant interaction between environmental information, long-term memory, and working memory has a direct impact on how we learn. Learning both uses existing understanding as a foundation and transforms it. The National Research Council summarizes in *How People Learn*:[3]

> **All learning involves transfer from previous experiences.... Effective teachers attempt to support positive transfer by actively identifying the strengths that students bring to a learning situation and building on them, thereby building bridges between students' knowledge and the learning objectives set out by the teacher.**

Product developers and marketers get all excited about turning their customers into content co-creators, but education's customers have always co-created their own learning.

Tactics for how we learn

Abandoning traditional broadcast-style, one-to-many lectures may be the most important tactic for aligning with how humans learn.

The real goal of a lecture should be to help students teach themselves. To support that, a lecturer needs to, as much as possible, present work in a fashion and language appropriate to their students' culture. This can be limited to pre-lecture research, but a more aggressive adjustment of the lecture model will likely be more effective, especially for small- to medium-size classes.

Some lecturers already include heavy interaction with students in their programs. While this practice may have started as a way to increase student engagement, its greatest value is the grounding in students' experiences it provides for lecture content.

Traditional lectures may become a specialty item when this transformation is taken to its logical extreme, used only to create some context for unfamiliar topics or to present a singular point of view that students would never have heard on their own.

---

3   National Research Council. *How People Learn*. National Academy Press, Washington, D.C., 2000, pg. 236.

Successful lectures

So now that we have blown up the traditional lecture model, as the smoke clears, what specific attributes of successful lectures should remain? Every lecture is part of the larger educational experience, so before we can explore key features, let's first describe the context in which a lecture might now exist.

Context

Liz Danzico, chair for the Interaction Design master's program at the School of Visual Arts in New York City, has seen the value of the lecture as a tool for delivering content diminish. It has been replaced by formats that better encourage two-way communication between instructors and students. In her program, lectures now play a supporting role for other educational tools:

> **The lecture establishes a point of view. It establishes a framework for people to understand what the scope or the spectrum of the conversation will be. With that framing device, you're then able to delve into informal conversation or some sort of activities. An opening lecture kind of greases the wheel.**

If lectures are grease in New York City, they are glue in Ohio. Karl Fast, an assistant professor for Kent State University's Information Architecture and Knowledge Management master's program, says:

> **A lecture isn't always just about the transfer of information. I mean it certainly is that, but I tend to approach this as the supplemental piece, the glue piece that connects the stuff that students have read and the things that I've had them do to come to class and the things that we're going to work on in class.**

The role of the lecturer also is part of a lecture's context. An instructor teaching the same course over a number of years may stick with a lecture over several semesters or quarters, using it to gauge the evolving reactions of students moving through the program.

An instructor responsible for a single course may use a lecture to tie the class into a larger program or take an approach similar to Karl Fast's, where no piece of the course, including a lecture, stands alone.

A guest speaker is more likely to revert to a more traditional approach to lectures and one-to-many communication. (They should fight that urge, however. They carry the same responsibility as the course's regular instructor to stimulate thinking by building bridges to the students' existing knowledge.)

Attributes of a successful lecture

Liz Danzico says that her program at the School of Visual Arts has redefined the measures of success for lectures:

> Betty Crocker in the 1950s wanted to look at how to raise the sales of their cake mixes. They determined that if they allowed people to add an egg to the cake mix it gave them more investment in the cake. If you think about a lecture in that way, it's not a predetermined set of instructions or a recipe, right? It's an opportunity or an invitation to participate.

It is less about demoting lectures and more about putting the student, rather than the curriculum, at the center of the educational experience. It is about an approach to lecturing that aligns with the way students think and learn. Within that environment, successful lectures must be:

- Flexible
- Reflective
- Connective
- Engaging
- Enthusiastic

Flexibility

Students should be able to trust the lecturer to cover the content they need to be successful for a class. Strong and obvious planning is essential to gaining student trust, but because learning builds on a foundation of existing student knowledge, that planning has to adjust when opportunities for deeper involvement arise.

Razorfish's Samantha Starmer taught courses for the University of Washington for seven years:

> You may find that you do a section and you think you're going to complete this whole piece you want to get across, but the students either aren't getting it or they're going off in a different direction that you can tell is really important to them, so you need to be very flexible on the fly.

Keys to flexibility

- Craft a detailed agenda so the impact of adjustments can be determined quickly.

- Develop a clear understanding of the lesson's key points that must tie into larger course concepts and milestones.

- Display an openness to tweaking process and content to tailor it more effectively to the students' needs.

Reflectiveness

Regardless of whether a lecture has been presented before, every class should somehow reflect the backgrounds and needs of the students in the room. Different students will respond differently to a class and it is the lecturer's job to do the adjusting.

The lecturer should seek out opportunities where students provide the core information in class conversations. Feedback from an instructor can be useful, but its value pales in comparison to students seeing how their peers approached a challenge they themselves had struggled with.

When a lecturing opportunity extends over several sessions, the instructor gets the chance to learn the personality of the group.

"You learn how much they want to be sharing their own examples or participating in exercises versus having you more formally teach them," says Starmer.

Keys for reflecting the class's personality

- Study the class's response as a group and as individuals.
- Find elements of the students' backgrounds that are directly relevant to course content.

Connectivity

Students should be able to easily understand where a specific lecture fits within the larger course concepts. They should have a sense of where the course will take them next. Every step forward through the content should feel like a continuation of the previous step.

Keys to connectivity

- Restate milestones met throughout a class and throughout the course.
- Cover key content despite the variations that occur.

Engagement

A student who is fully engaged with a lesson can be a viral agent that infects other students who might otherwise mentally wander away. They help translate content both with their questions and by the statements they make in class. Their reactions can help the lecturer measure class response to content.

Karen McGrane, managing partner at Bond Art and Science and an instructor for the School of Visual Arts in New York City, drives engagement by relying on student content:

> My job is so much easier if they ask a lot of questions. My job is so much easier if, when I give them case studies to work on, everybody comes back with some things to say. I personally learn so much more by giving them problems to solve: "I want to give you this scenario and I want to hear how you would solve it." The process of hearing what they think about it and how they work through some of the issues is really enlightening for me.

Keys to engagement

- Give people their own way to discover something that will make it mean more.

- Let student questions guide the lecture rather than forcing the class back to the original content.

Enthusiasm

The lecturer should be able to display interest and accurately read the interest of the class. Karl Fast notes:

> **One of the things that students seem highly attuned to is when you walk into the room and you're just going through the motions. Even when you've got lots of different slides, and you really know your stuff, I find that there's a really important element where you still have to come across as "I am giving this for you."**

And while a caffeinated interest can buoy the class for short periods of time, intellectual curiosity about the subject is more powerful and longer lasting.

Keys to enthusiasm

- Let humor and informality lighten a tense or tired room.

- Find genuine opportunities to show excitement.

Deck/no deck

Is a PowerPoint or Keynote slide deck an essential element of a successful lecture? Educators have had differing experiences on the topic.

"I have had to accept for myself that, if I'm giving a lecture, slides with bullet points on them are perfectly acceptable and even expected. Coming from doing so much conference speaking where I would never, ever stand up in front of a group of people with a slide with bullet points on it...I sometimes feel like, 'No! I need to have slides with pictures of cats on them.'" —Karen McGrane

"In my classroom lectures, I try to use as few visuals as possible. I've noticed in a classroom that if you have a slide deck it actually disengages the conversation. It feels formal to people and they don't want to interrupt. It tells people there will be something to look at later so they don't have to pay attention." —Dave Malouf

"Having some structure with slides helps me know where I'm at." —Samantha Starmer

"Someone comes to a conversation with slides and it's like, 'This is what I think. I don't know what you think, but this is what I have to tell you.' There's something limiting about that." —Liz Danzico

Why teach?

Lecturers may be tempted to craft lessons in PowerPoint that pound bullet points into their students' brains. This is a bad approach that is doomed to frustration and failure. Educators like Liz Danzico and Dave Malouf are rethinking the structure of education. They want to remove content from the position of primacy and replace it with the students' experience. They have pushed the traditional lecturing model aside and replaced it with a variety of models, all intended to create real conversations that bring their students' backgrounds into the learning.

It is a challenging time to be an instructor. Teaching, especially teaching one or more full courses, is extremely difficult and time intensive.

The personal fulfillment felt when helping others attracts some to teaching, but for practicing user experience professionals, the opportunity to extend their own skills is the more powerful effect. Dave Malouf explains:

I've learned more about design since being a teacher than in the 15 years before being a teacher. It's just been exponential. It's not just the classroom, it's also the engagement from peers, but the combination has brought about an exponential rise in learning about myself, learning about design, learning about business. I feel more connected to my own culture when I'm teaching.

A successful lecture gets students to learn by first getting them to think. For generations, educators treated their students like empty vessels in need of filling, but education in the twenty-first century is focused more and more on aligning with how human thinking actually works.

Post-Facilitation

When you've wrapped up all the facilitation activities you spent so much time planning and preparing for, it can be easy to forget that there's still more to be done. While it's still fresh in everyone's mind, let your participants or audience pick your brain and learn more about the content, and solicit feedback from them about the information you provided and how you performed. Then you can pack up your belongings and head out the door.

Chapter 18

Managing Q&A

He must be very ignorant for he answers
every question he is asked.

— Voltaire

I went to the doctor, I went to the mountains
I looked to the children, I drank from the fountain
There's more than one answer to these questions
Pointing me in crooked line
The less I seek my source for some definitive
The closer I am to fine.

— The Indigo Girls

There's a Zen parable that goes as follows:

> **Upon meeting a Zen master at a social event, a psychiatrist asked him a question that had been on his mind.**
>
> **"Exactly how do you help people?" he inquired.**
>
> **"I get them where they can't ask any more questions," the master answered.**

It's unlikely that this particular Zen master ever met a four-year-old or the designer who was following the path of why. Regardless of how thorough your planning and preparation are, you're likely to be asked a question that requires you to provide more detail on a subject. Fret not—this is natural. Participants may have their own views into the information you presented, and their frame of reference may provide a perspective you hadn't previously considered.

When you're doing your research for your presentation, you'll probably collect more information than you could hope to share in your session. Part of your task is to winnow the content down to a point where it will get the key messages across and fit into the allotted time frame. You'll inevitably encounter questions, but hopefully your preparation and planning will provide you with enough knowledge to answer them.

Simple rules to dating my Q&A

It's pretty easy to fall into the trap of preparing and planning only for the material you need to present and facilitate. The reality is that there's much more to facilitating than providing information, eliciting responses, and guiding participants. You also need to manage any inbound questions and provide a response that will keep the session moving.

By taking on the role of facilitator, you're self-identifying as an expert. You may be the expert on the topic at hand, or the expert who knows how to lead a group toward a goal, but you'll be the expert.

As the expert, you can expect to be viewed as the person who holds most of, if not all, the answers. How you handle those questions and the people who ask them will show off your skills as a facilitator. Use the following guidelines to help you on your way.

Dos

Set the Q&A rules up front. As the facilitator, you define the rules of engagement and it's up to you (and your host, if you have one) to make sure the participants are aware of your intentions. Let them know if you'll be taking questions as you go, after the session, or not at all in order to mitigate unwanted interruptions.

Know your topic. The most important thing you can do is to be prepared and have the knowledge you need to accomplish the goals you've set for your session. The more prepared you are, the more likely it is that you'll be able to answer questions related to the topic, or at least be able to provide guidance and direction toward a solution.

Repeat the question. Restating a question allows you to clarify your understanding and formulate a response. Literal repetition isn't necessary; you should feel free to paraphrase in order to simplify and clarify what's being asked of you.

Provide incentives for being engaged. Some authors have been known to share copies of their books with people who ask questions during their sessions. Others provide snacks or other rewards for those who want to play a more active role. A little "chumming of the water" may inspire your participants to pay close attention to the session.

Be aware of the time. If the questions are presented to you in the middle of a session, you are likely on the clock. Your plans and schedule can quickly get derailed if you spend too much time answering questions. If you're one person among a group scheduled to facilitate, be respectful of the others' time and make sure you allow them enough time to get prepared and be ready to start. Watch the clock, and respond accordingly and with respect. Questions can always be answered at another time and via another medium.

Provide a way to continue the conversation. This requires a bit more planning, but if you're able to direct participants to another way to continue the Q&A, you'll do everyone a great service. You can prepare a blog post about the content beforehand and allow people to further engage you at a later time, or create a discussion forum where participants can engage you as well as other participants. If you're able to share slides or similar content, post them to a slide-sharing service such as SlideShare (http://slideshare.net) and let the discussion continue there. And, of course, be prepared to share your email address, Twitter handle, or other contact information.

Don'ts

Be afraid of not knowing the answer. It happens—you can't plan for every question that will come up, and it's OK to admit you don't know an answer. When this happens, simply own it, take a note, and let the person who asked know that you'll be happy to follow up after the session.

Let someone else take control. A participant will sometimes start to tell you a long-winded story or personal anecdote rather than getting right to his or her question.

When you sense this happening, politely interrupt and ask the participant to skip ahead to the question so that others can have an opportunity to ask their questions or so you can keep on schedule.

Feel compelled to answer every question right now. Sometimes the answer you need to give may require some additional research on your part. Or you might not be certain if you have the right answer. Or you may get a question that's so far out of bounds or off topic that it doesn't make sense to spend time answering it in the time you have available. When this happens, politely refuse the question and provide the participant with a reason for moving on, as well as an opportunity for follow-up at a later time.

Provide an environment for doing battle. It's rare, but sometimes people will not agree with you. You can foster a healthy discussion where both sides find a way to compromise, change views, or agree to disagree. But, if the tone gets combative, no one wins. As the facilitator, it's your job to keep an eye on the barometer and avoid stormy weather at all costs. It's far better to politely move on to a different question than to spend time in verbal swordplay; you risk losing far more than a battle of words.

Force, or feel obligated to engage in Q&A. In fact, don't be afraid to not have Q&A at all. There is no requirement that you have Q&A. Cennydd Bowles, a product designer at Twitter, takes the "Sorry, No Questions" approach, and prefers to answer questions in a different venue and not immediately after a presentation.

Meet the Expert: Cennydd Bowles

Cennydd Bowles is a product designer at Twitter, and author of the book *Undercover User Experience Design.*

I believe it's important to let a speaker talk with her audience after a session, but there has to be a better way. A speaker should decline onstage questions. Instead, she should tell her audience where they can find her to talk in person, ideally immediately afterward. She can then truly listen, and discuss the issues without the onstage pressures that reward sound bites over insight.

"Sorry, No Questions" is my preferred policy for public speaking. If it's something you'd like to be part of, please join in and spread the word. If it's not for you, that's fine. I'll do my part to ask only meaningful questions.

Post Q&A

When the Q&A is done, the conversation doesn't have to end, and in many cases, it's time for new conversations to start. Don't shy away from taking more questions and continuing the discussion after the session is over. Every question that's presented to you is an opportunity for you not only to use all that knowledge you acquired during planning and preparation, but also to consider possibilities you might not have thought of.

Meet the Expert: Adam Polansky

Adam Polansky is a UX strategist at Bottle Rocket and a faculty member of Cranky Talk Workshops.

•

You never know where discussions may lead. Even if two people feel the need to keep it going over a cup of coffee or a discussion group, there's no limit to the effects over time. The most successful companies in history and entire communities of practice emerged from a single, astute, shared observation.

On a modest scale, someone might take a risk, change jobs, solve an old problem, or simply change the way they do something and be a little happier. As the storyteller, you're the catalyst for the discussion. But don't stop there. Give that discussion traction to keep it alive.

Adam Polansky is right. It's unlikely that you'll ever have enough time to get all of your participants to the Zen-like point of being unable to ask any more questions, so use that to your advantage. The more you discuss a topic, the more likely you are to find new opportunities to learn about it.

Chapter 19

Measuring Success

Success consists of going from failure to
failure without loss of enthusiasm.

— Winston Churchill

The ultimate goal of any facilitation is to support the success of a larger effort.
Unfortunately, it can be difficult to accurately connect the results of a brainstorming exercise, kickoff meeting, or mentoring session to the overall success
of a project. So, ideally, every facilitation effort will include a way to measure its
own effectiveness.

Different types of facilitation have different measures, but the one thing you can
count on is that each effort offers the facilitator an opportunity to learn and grow.
To take advantage of those opportunities, however, you have to pay attention.

Here's a fairy tale to illustrate the point.

Once upon a time

A talented princess named Tangerine Blossom quit her job in Big City, sold all of her
worldly possessions, and used the money to buy a three-room bungalow in Mountain View, a magical land of angels, unicorns, and code monkeys.

Tangerine made the move west to study at the feet of a legendary guru who had launched a start-up there way, way back in the First Age of Internet. Semiretired and fabulously wealthy, the guru had a reputation for transforming ambitious acolytes into highly successful professionals.

"Why are you here, my dear?" the guru asked Tangerine on the first day of her low-paying internship.

"Master, I want to know the secret to success."

The guru chuckled quietly to himself and told Tangerine to walk toward the nearest mountain for 30 minutes and report back the next morning on whether or not she saw the mountain move during her trek.

Tangerine meets her guru.

For the entire 30-minute walk, Tangerine kept her eyes fixed on the mountain. She ignored the people and activities around her and tried hard not to blink, worried she might miss something important.

The next morning she entered the guru's gigantic corner office with a sad expression clouding her face.

"What is it, child?" the guru asked.

"I failed, Master. I didn't see the mountain move."

The guru told her to spend that entire morning walking toward the nearest mountain, checking for movement. Again, she did so without allowing anything to distract her. And again she walked into the guru's office the next morning crestfallen.

"I did not see the mountain move, Master."

"Did you get a milkshake at Moe's, the diner just outside of town?" the guru asked.

"Should I, Master? Will it unlock the great mysteries of success?"

"Well, I don't know about that, but they do make a pretty good milkshake. In any case, tomorrow I would like you to spend the full day, from sunup to sundown, walking toward the mountain."

Checking the mountain for movement.

Again, Tangerine did as the guru commanded. She ignored the activity around her as she walked and decided not to stop for a milkshake in fear that she might miss something important. At the end of the day, she turned around and it took her all night to make her way back. Exhausted, she dragged herself into the guru's office again.

"I have failed you, Master," she said. "I will not, in any way, question your great wisdom or doubt your mysterious ways, but I have to ask: Will the mountain eventually move?"

The guru took a long draw from his can of Diet Mountain Dew and then replied:

"What, are you kidding? Mountains move constantly. Didn't you ever hear of plate tectonics? Geez, what do they teach you people in college these days?

"I, I, uh ...," Tangerine stuttered.

"Look, pal," the guru said, "if you spend all your time so focused on success, you're going to do a lot of walking for nothing."

Successful outcomes

As Tangerine Blossom saw, focusing solely on measurable success can be foolish. The effort you put into orchestrating a complex conversation should enrich your life in some way. For everybody else, you'll have to provide something more tangible. Consider the suggested approaches below.

Brainstorming

Brainstorming is the generation and evolution of ideas by a diverse group of individuals. Brainstorming's dependence on the unfettered creativity of the group makes it essential that every exercise begin with a concrete, specific definition of the problem to be addressed.

Is a product in danger of losing market share? Are there processes that need fixing? Does new functionality need to be explored?

Once the problem has been defined, a set of goals can be created to give the facilitator something to measure against after the session. If a product is losing market share, for example, the goals might be:

- Generate and prioritize a list of new features.
- Describe disruptions in the market.
- Create a stronger product.

Goal definition should inform the invitation list and help the facilitator select the most effective activities to run during the session.

In smaller organizations (or groups isolated within larger organizations), it may be relatively easy to manage the team that defines the problem and outlines goals. But in big organizations, many people often get involved in the definition process and that can lead to a real mess.

The facilitator may be tempted to keep her head down and focus on the details of running the session rather than getting sucked into the corporate maelstrom. But a duck-and-cover response to politics and bureaucracy risks sacrificing the value of the effort and that can end up threatening the facilitator's credibility.

Frequently, a facilitator has to take it upon herself to make room in an organization for her work. Left to their own devices, many companies will treat brainstorming as silly fun or one of a series of checklist items. Neither description will result in true success for brainstorming.

Contextual inquiry

Mark Twain taught us:

> **If you hold a cat by the tail you learn things you cannot learn any other way.**

Like holding a cat by its tail, contextual inquiry yields unique data, and that makes it a bit tricky to measure success. Viewing people in their own environments often provides teams with unexpected information. So how can you plan measurement around surprises?

One approach is to assess the effect of the facilitator on the individuals they study. When subjects are put at ease, they lower their defenses and provide both a higher volume and variety of information. The investigator can also show success by defining the relationships between subjects and by thoroughly cataloging the details of the subjects' work environment.

Ultimately, contextual inquiry is part of a larger user-research effort and its success is strongly tied to the success of the overall research. User research pays off for the organization when products and services are popular with target audiences and easily used and understood by primary users.

Focus groups

Focus groups collect subjective answers to subjective questions in order to provide organizations with data that can be interpreted strategically.

Billions of dollars have been spent on bringing strangers together in groups and asking them questions about services and products. Unfortunately, a big reason why people authorize budgets for focus groups is because the results are so flexible. A skilled executive can interpret focus group data almost any way she pleases. If the level of that executive's satisfaction is treated as the primary measure of success, it corrupts any legitimate assessment of the focus group.

Gauging the quality of the facilitator's interaction with the group is a more useful measurement. The facilitator should minimize the impact of the group dynamic, which, left unchecked, can threaten the validity of data. The facilitator should cover the required material, but do so in a way that participants feel they are contributing to a genuine conversation. Finally, a successful facilitator should, as much as possible, enable participants to forget the artificiality of the session.

Interviews

For any one-on-one conversation, success is based on the quality of the data collected. Interviewers strive for factual and insightful comments from their interviewees. Objectivity is valued as well, with information that reflects little to none of the interviewer's influence.

In many cases, specific artifacts (key quotes, process flows, video clips, and so on) can be identified as expected outcomes and help measure an interview's success, as can the analysis of patterns that emerge from multiple interviews.

Kickoff meetings

The enthusiasm and confidence of attendees is a good measure of the short-term success of the first meeting of a project's full team. Longer-term success is harder to gauge. When essential information is poorly communicated in kickoff meetings, the damage might not be seen until well into the project as different team members discover different expectations among the group.

A successful kickoff meeting provides enough information to gain credibility for the project, but not so much that the information overwhelms the participants.

Lectures

Colleges, universities, and trade schools have embraced the collection of performance reviews, but they tend to be gathered only at the end of the semester. Without getting in your employer's way, you can introduce simple surveys that provide data for analysis over time, for example, by asking students to rate your performance in key categories every four weeks.

While the traditional focus of teacher-student meetings has been on the progress of the student, you can experiment with questions about your progress as well.

Peer feedback can play a role. In the spirit of design critiques, you can invite a more experienced educator to sit in on a lecture to provide feedback.

Websites for rating teachers exist, but they tend to have low participation without the direct support of the school.

Mentoring

Defining expectations at the start of a mentoring relationship gives both parties something to measure the partnership against over time, as does the regular creation and fulfillment of smaller action items along the way.

Ultimately, those who receive mentoring decide which advice to take and which advice to set aside. Some mentoring relationships are no longer than a single interaction, while others last for entire careers. So perhaps the only credible measure of mentoring success is its ability to inspire each generation of mentees to mentor others. That kind of success is most in line with the core intent and value of mentoring.

Panels

Measuring success with panels is quite a bit easier than with other kinds of conversations for the simple reason that most panels suck. They come by their mediocrity honestly: With no panelist wanting to step on other panelists' toes and limited exposure to the full panel during planning, most panels are really three or four mini-presentations in disguise.

Those little arcs usually require clumsy transitions between speakers and make effective rhythm impossible. And the format means that most of the time, panelists are sitting patiently instead of entering into an interesting discussion.

Successful panels are arguments. While this may be uncomfortable for panelists, it can be fascinating for the audience. Watching smart people argue about interesting things more directly stimulates the audience's brains than even the best orchestrated mini-presentations.

A successful moderator puts the pieces in place so that most of the panelists' time is spent talking, and arguing, with other panelists (and sometimes the audience). Interaction is more important than expertise and vastly more important than etiquette.

Participatory design

Problem definition is the key to measuring the success of sessions where users are active participants in the design process. First, identify a problem for which participatory design is the right solution. Then, determine what aspect of the problem this specific instance of participatory design should address.

With a solid problem definition in place, the quality of the design solutions created can be a measure of the session's success. Including users as codesigners is a sizable investment, so organizations should demand ambitious results whenever participatory design is attempted.

Presentations

Unlike classroom settings where students and lecturers build relationships over time, relatively little is known about the audience for a presentation at a conference or similar public event. As a result, measuring the success of presentations is different than measuring the success of lectures.

If you've ever Googled yourself, you have a sense of both the attraction and the danger of sites like SpeakerRate.com. Soon after giving a talk, you can see what people thought of your performance and content. The positive aspect is the variety and transparency of the ratings; the negative is that it can make you very aware of where you fall on the obsessive-compulsive spectrum as you go back on a daily basis to see how you've been judged.

A better approach is to build success measurement into your presentation preparation. There's no substitute for the data you get by running through your full talk in front of a small audience of more experienced speakers. Starting a review and revise cycle weeks before your public presentation gives you plenty of time for multiple rounds and is the best measure of your success. Armed with full knowledge of your strongest and weakest stuff, you can usually analyze the response of the audience on the big day.

And then log in to SpeakerRate.com, because really, can you help yourself?

Sales calls

You might expect that getting the sale is the ultimate measure of success. But the sale is just an early stage of a longer relationship with the client—it's the relationship that has the real value. So any tracking of client retention is a relevant gauge.

Depth of knowledge (about the project, the potential client, and possibly the industry) is a healthier measure of success for an individual conversation. It puts less pressure on you during the sales call itself and gives you more information to work with later. If, instead of talking about yourself for an hour, you took part in a meaningful conversation where the clients learned about you and you learned about them, then you couldn't have been more successful.

Usability testing

You might think the success of usability testing would lead directly to a reduction of defects or some creative measure of a product's usability. But successful usability testing doesn't always answer questions. In fact, the more questions it raises, and the earlier it raises them, the more successful it can be considered.

The success of usability testing should be measured by a combination of the clarity of insights presented in the analysis of the testing, the impact of recommendations on actual development, and the product's overall success.

Virtual seminars

The original tagline for director Ridley Scott's movie *Alien* was "In space, no one can hear you scream." Virtual seminars can feel just like the silent vacuum of space. It's easy to derail yourself as you're presenting, thinking about your audience with their phones or computers on mute and their minds lost in a dozen other tasks while you try to give the greatest performance of your life.

The measure of success for virtual seminars can be as simple as someone asking you to do another one. There are also basic measures of efficiency, for example, that you started and ended on time and that you didn't do anything to screw up your phone and computer connections during the presentation.

Workshops

Workshops are probably the most robust type of facilitation for collecting measures of success. They are complex, intense experiences for everyone involved. As the designer of that experience, you can build success measurement right into the program. Running a group success or improvement conversation for ten minutes at the end of the workshop can provide great insights into your work. You can also conduct surveys where participants rate based on categories using a scale of one to five. These are wonderful ways to collect quantitative feedback that you can compare across multiple workshops.

Because workshops tend to build personal relationships between all involved, you can also follow the session with one-on-one interviews in the days following the event.

Happily ever after

Eventually, Tangerine Blossom got her guru's point and learned to enjoy the journey. As she facilitated a wide variety of conversations, she started to take her personal measures of success at least as seriously as her organization treated its own.

Then, after years of promotions and success, she took all that she learned back to Big City where she lived (and worked) happily ever after.

Chapter 20

Horror Stories

From even the greatest of horrors
irony is seldom absent.

— H. P. Lovecraft

All the planning and practice in the world can't prepare you for the unknown. This holds true when it comes to facilitation, too! Eventually, you'll find yourself in a situation that you never dreamt possible, with little time to react or solve the problem. Sometimes you just have to suck it up, go with the flow, and pray that you can complete your presentation and come out unscathed.

Horror stories from the field

We asked several brilliant people to share their stories about situations that were less than perfect. Enough time has passed that they're able to laugh about their experiences. You should laugh, too, and hopefully learn from them.

Steve Baty

Principal, Meld Studios

Steve Baty is a founder and principal of Meld Studios, president of the Interaction Design Association (IxDA), founder of the UX Book Club, and co-chair of the UX Australia conference series.

Sixteen years ago I was looking after the launch of a new version of Freehand (Macromedia at the time) into Australia. I was working as the product manager for the local distributor, and the Macromedia Users Group in Melbourne had arranged for me to fly down to give them a sneak peek of the new software.

Illustration and print software was still pretty big news in 1996 and the event had sold out—about 150 people. It was the headline event of the calendar for the group. They'd been talking about it for months.

I left Sydney around 3:00 p.m. armed with an external hard drive loaded up with a release candidate version of the software and a bunch of demo files. I'd given the demo a few times already and spent a lot of hours working with the software in beta (I was an active member of the beta testing community)—I was as well prepared as I could be. The flight to Melbourne took an hour—typical, uneventful.

The event was due to begin at 6:30 and I arrived at 5:30, in plenty of time. They were still setting up, so I spent some time chatting with folks as they arrived. At around 6:15, I took my hard drive over to the computer we were using for the event—you couldn't really run something like Freehand on a laptop back in those days, not fast, anyway.

I plugged it into the computer. Plugged in the power cord. Turned it on.

And it burst into flames.

It burst. . . into. . . flames.

And took the software with it.

I had no backup with me. No CD. Nothing.

The room was very, very quiet. (After the fire was put out at least.)

And then I spent 90 minutes giving a verbal demonstration of Freehand. I answered questions about old bugs that had been fixed. I talked about new features that had been added. And I couldn't show them a damn thing.

I have never—ever—turned up to a talk since without at least one, sometimes two or three, alternative ways of giving that presentation.

Sunni Brown

Founder and Creative Director of sunnibrown.com

Sunni Brown is an international speaker and author who runs a visual-thinking consultancy. She is also the leader of the Doodle Revolution, a global campaign for visual literacy.

I wouldn't go so far as to say I was horrified by the experience I'm about to describe, but it certainly presented a challenge that required me to be very present and skillful with the group. Groups can be wily creatures; this instance kept me on my toes.

I was partnering with a large company and a small team within that company. One of the goals of the session was to help the team move toward higher performance, together. I described some of the characteristics of high-performance teams (trust, commitment, responsibility) and when I arrived at the characteristic of "facing areas of weakness," one of the group members started to cry. Right there in the middle of the meeting, with some discretion but certainly not enough to go unnoticed.

This was a first for me as a facilitator so, having no clear path to take, I resorted to instinct. I wanted to compassionately acknowledge her state of being while simultaneously not allowing it to disrupt the progress of the whole group. I would not have that same response every time someone cried in a meeting—there's certainly an opportunity for a group breakthrough there—but it was clear to me in that moment that (a) her crying or emotional instability at work was not unusual, (b) members of the team, having experienced her emotional reactions before, were not in a space to accommodate her, or even to be curious, and (c) the struggle was personal and not specific to the dynamics of the group. So I thought that the best opportunity I had with her would be one-on-one. I deduced all of this in a nanosecond, subconsciously, so my assessment could very well have been inaccurate.

I turned toward the woman and said, "It looks like some part of this conversation has triggered you. Would you be open to sharing some of what's coming up for you outside of the group setting?" She seemed relieved to be acknowledged but not asked to divulge, and she excused herself from the room. I closed the current conversation with the remainder of the group and asked for a 10-minute break. During the break, the woman was forthcoming about some of her struggles and asked for my advice. I told her the following things:

Emotional responses to life are healthy and normal.

She was a strong and capable human being who was struggling, like all of us do at various times.

Her display of emotion was courageous and, in the long run, preferable to repressing how she felt.

There was an opportunity for her to discover parts of herself that were creating consistent obstacles in her work and personal life, and she could learn to deal with those parts wisely and compassionately.

I recommended that she stay with us throughout the remainder of the process because her contribution had been valuable and because she was part of their team. But I also asked that she interpret her behavior as a signal of distress that she would be served by attending to in earnest. I gave her a hug (the best medicine next to laughter), then gave her some frameworks that I know to be helpful in discerning and managing difficult behavior. I also had a debrief with her manager after the entire session ended, to get more context and to support the manager who was, naturally, also experiencing turmoil relative to this team member.

Clearly, I wasn't hired for group therapy and I would have been ridiculously out of my league to try and play that role. But I wasn't ruffled (thankfully) by the emergence of spontaneous human emotions and I tried to handle them like a connected, caring group leader who was balancing an obligation to move toward an outcome. I know that people don't leave their selves behind when they go to work. We sometimes try, but there's only so much of our selves we can avoid. This experience reinforced my sense of responsibility as a facilitator and reminded me that when we go into a setting with real people, we never know what we're going to find. So I come with as much preparation and presence as I can, and consider the rest to be education the group gives me.

Dave Malouf

Principal, Dave Malouf Design & Co-founder, Peer Loft

Dave Malouf is an observer and pattern recognizer who co-founded Peer Loft to create products and services that help teams amplify their creativity.

When I think of all the scary, horrible moments of having a disaster happen while I'm presenting, there's one that jumps to the top of the list every time. It epitomizes the perfect storm of everything going wrong on a presentation, all of which is completely outside your control.

I was giving a talk at the Holon Institute of Technology (HIT) on a rather warm (even for Israel) March day. I had already given a half-day workshop that morning that went kinda bleh and had to rush across metro Tel Aviv using only my iPhone GPS. Let's just say that the Israeli highway system can be unforgiving if you don't know exactly where you're going.

I finally made it to HIT, but then I had to find where I had to go. My two years of living in Israel 15 years ago seemed useless given how little I retained of my Hebrew speaking and, more importantly, reading skills. Just by accident I found the right building and my very gracious host. The time between the previous day and that day was a very stressful prelude to going on stage and it only got worse.

The event started in a nice auditorium. I was the second-to-last speaker—basically the warm-up act for one of my favorite designers and thinkers in the world, Nathan Shedroff. Have you ever performed in front of an idol? Yeah, that feeling.

The woman who spoke before me went on and had her own disaster occur. The screen went blank and the projector shut off. Apparently the room was too hot and the projector auto-shut off because it overheated. I forget how they helped her finish her talk, but it ended a bit late and I had a fixed ending because I had to head across town to my next talk.

We had to wait a bit before I went on. What were they doing? They turned the air conditioning as high as it would go, basically transforming the room into a small beer locker. I thought, "At least the audience won't be falling asleep anytime soon."

Finally, I went on. Things were going great. I was in the zone. All the previous stress washed away and I was giving probably one of my best presentations on a topic I'd never given before. I was about 40 slides into my 80-slide presentation, when suddenly my slides wouldn't go forward. I could go back. But I couldn't go forward.

I tried jumping to a later slide and it wouldn't work either. I tried all manner of fixery. I tried recopying it to a jump drive. Anything.

At this point you need to understand that the deck was near 1GB because it had a lot of embedded video (because you can't rely on Internet connections). So transfers and copies were taking a long time. Mind you, I had a lot of video because, well, I had to show people what I was talking about. I couldn't just talk about it, or so I thought.

Some good people took on the challenge of getting my slides together. So I was caught in the ultimate time-stretch performance of my life. For what felt like an eternity but was probably closer to 10 to 15 minutes, I gave my presentation without a single slide.

I'm a good performer. I don't show my nerves on stage a lot, but I was shivering with fear this time around and everyone in the audience saw it and was paralyzed with horror on my behalf. About two minutes into this slideless period, I surveyed the audience, took a deep breath, and said, "Loosen up, you all look so nervous."

The crowd broke out in laughter. We all relaxed and until the computer was back in action again, I did great. The audience remained engaged. I entertained and I communicated clearly and articulately what I needed to. It's like the slides were there all along, but also like they were completely unnecessary. The pictures were painted to satisfaction with my words and movements.

They returned a computer to me and I finished my talk, trying to get in as many of the videos as possible. But I had to finish on time, so I never really got through the whole talk.

What did I learn from this experience?

Put your presentations on drives and Dropbox, regardless of size.

Create platform-independent versions of your presentation. For me that has meant having both Keynote and PDF or QuickTime versions of my presentations, depending on whether or not I have video embedded.

Have a sense of humor that is both self-deprecating and appropriately sarcastic. This is very useful when you're in a bind during a performance.

Rehearse until you can give your talk without your slides.

Slides are truly unnecessary. In fact, in my institutional teaching I don't use slides that much at all since this event.

Remain calm. No one ever died of embarrassment. And no audience of professionals ever killed a presenter for a computer crashing on them halfway through a presentation.

The fallout of the experience was that I had two days to find a new laptop, as I was giving a full-day workshop and had to find a way to present for that. I did and everything went fine in the end.

I still feel I need to go back to Israel and vindicate my performance. I'm sure I'll get a chance soon.

Eric L. Reiss

CEO, The FatDUX Group

A seasoned presenter and the author of several books, Eric Reiss heads a leading user-experience design company, headquartered in Copenhagen, Denmark.

I gave a keynote on intranets a few years ago that was very well received—so well, in fact, that I was asked to give variations at several other conferences. Based on several glowing recommendations, I was flown to Paris to address a small, highly select group of intranet professionals.

The organizer of the summit told me, "Don't be afraid to challenge us. Make us think. Don't hold back." And I didn't—with dire results.

It soon became clear that these people were actually pretty touchy and few were interested in any truth that wasn't exceptionally well varnished. I naturally adjusted my tone and message accordingly. Things were almost back on track— there were a few laughs, there were many smiles—when suddenly an audience member yelled out that this just wasn't the way *he* did things. I was about to respond when the organizer answered for me. To my horror, he twisted my viewpoints to fit his personal agenda, setting off a raging discussion, which he led with depressing gusto. For over 10 minutes, I could barely get a word in edgewise.

When I was finally allowed to continue my presentation, it was clear that whatever rapport I had built up, however slight it may have been, was gone forever. Later, the organizer told me I was one of the worst speakers they had ever had.

He was probably right.

Kate Niederhoffer

Kate Niederhoffer, Founder, Knowable Research

Kate Niederhoffer founded Knowable Research to bring the rigor of social science to business. She blogs occasionally at socialabacus.blogspot.com and is on Twitter @katenieder.

Peter Kim

Peter Kim, VP Managing Director, R/GA

Peter Kim is a management consultant, industry analyst, and coauthor of Social Business by Design. *He blogs at beingpeterkim.com and tweets as @peterkim.*

We had recently completed a major business strategy engagement for a multibillion dollar, publicly traded midwestern U.S. company. Our client-side sponsor and all relevant stakeholders had already signed off on the work, so we had one step left that was more of a formality than anything: present our findings to the CEO, COO, and cross-functional management team. Our team had no concerns about the content; we just had to take our executive summary deck and summarize a bit further, focus on business implications, and stay away from technical details, engaging the CEO and helping him feel good about his spend.

Presentation day arrived. This was actually our second meeting with the CEO. Our first meeting (at project inception) began with the CEO walking into the conference room and immediately circling around the table, adjusting each of the chairs to the same height. Only then were we able to introduce ourselves and discuss the project we had been hired to deliver. Now, as somewhat of a bookend, we were at the end of the engagement phase and ready to present findings and recommendations. The account executive on our side began the presentation with a high-level overview and quickly transitioned to our lead consultant. The presentation dynamic was choppy, as the COO constantly debated semantics that were at best a tertiary, maybe quaternary concern to our work. Then about halfway though the scheduled hour, it happened.

The CEO stood up from the table and walked over to a window near the front of the room, adjacent to the presenter. Our lead consultant gave a sideways look at the account executive; the junior consultant we had brought as a "learning experience" had eyes open as wide as a deer in headlights. But all of our clients had their eyes glued to the presenter, as if their CEO was nothing more than a janitor who simply picked an inopportune time to dust the blinds. The CEO had moved on to sniffing at the blinds, it seemed—or peeking through the tiny space between the slats. The lead consultant could barely keep a straight face. No one on the client side would acknowledge anything strange, let alone humorous. Laughs were fighting to emerge, making important-sounding summaries of our work impossible. The lead consultant gave a knowing glance to the account executive, who fluidly picked up the presentation in a commanding voice.

After a couple minutes, the CEO sat back down, wrote three lines on a yellow legal pad, slid it over to the COO, then stood up and walked out of the room with no further acknowledgement to anyone. Still, our clients had their eyes pointed forward as if this was an apparition only the consulting team could see. We finished the presentation and got approval to start on the next phase of work a couple weeks later.

No one knows what was written on that legal pad or what the blinds smelled like that day. What I've learned is that you can pre-seed findings, get briefed on political motivations, and make sure delivery is tight, but you still need to be prepared for anything. Be sure your team is adept at reading one another's body language and subtle facial expressions. Fluid transitions are key when you need to hold back raucous laughter at the expense of a budget-holding executive with a peculiar idiosyncrasy.

Donna Spencer

UX consultant and author

Donna Spencer is a freelance user experience designer who specializes in large, messy websites and business applications. She is an author of three books and runs the UX Australia conference.

My worst conference presentation was a few years ago at a small conference in Australia. I got up, put my lapel microphone on, introduced myself and the basic idea for the talk, and switched to the second slide. There were two photos on it, and as I stared at them I had no idea what they were about. No, the slide pixies didn't get in and add photos—I had put them there. I just couldn't remember what the photos were of or what I had intended to talk about. It slowly came back to me and I stumbled through, but it threw my confidence for the rest of the talk, and I was very unhappy with my presentation. I was stunned to later find out that it was not at all obvious to the room.

What had happened here? I did many simple things wrong! It was a new talk and I put it together in a rush around client work (which means I wasn't really concentrating properly). I didn't rehearse at all (I sort of ran through the story in my head as I wrote it, but didn't do it out loud). I went out late, slept badly, and woke tired.

I could have managed with the late night and lack of sleep had I rehearsed my talk out loud a couple of times. Rehearsing aloud means I can carry on with the story even if things go badly, because I've heard it before. I know what to say because I've heard myself say it before.

Now I always rehearse.

Nathan Shedroff

Program Chair, MBA in Design Strategy,
California College of the Arts

Nathan Shedroff is the chair of the groundbreaking MBA in Design Strategy at the California College of the Arts in San Francisco.

When I presented in Finland for the first time, the audience was absolutely stoic throughout. No one even cracked a smile, let alone a laugh. I pretty much knew my talk wasn't going over—to the point that I wondered if they could even understand English well. I shouldn't have worried. That reaction (or lack thereof) is a cultural artifact. As soon as I was done with my keynote, many people came up to me, animated, asking lots of questions, and congratulating me on the talk (at least they thought it was good). When I asked my host about the difference in my experience, he laughed. He said something like, "Oh, that's just the Finnish! We never ask questions and we never react. It's part of our upbringing. I should have warned you."

Humor is even more difficult, of course. I once had a joke in my slides (it was a slide of the senses, explaining how they related to interfaces and sensorial design, and I had listed Horse Sense, Common Sense, and one other—I can't even remember now). I didn't even realize it was in there, as I had used a GIF from another presentation and I would have changed it had I remembered. One of the audience members (from a European country) asked what these were. How do you describe an English-centric bad joke to someone who obviously didn't get it and, instead, thought it was something important?

Yeah, you don't.

Jason Kunesh

*Director of User Experience and
Product, Obama for America*

Jason Kunesh most recently performed as Director of User Experience and Product at Obama for America.

I was running an engagement with a major financial services company that was completing a merger with another financial services company. We had been hired to review the two banks' software, provide mentorship to their team members through workshops, and identify best practices to build on.

The two cultures couldn't have been more different even though they both were banks. One was from the southern East Coast, the other was from the West. The first sign that things were awry was when we met the teams at the kickoff and one of the team members kept swigging from a bottle of Pepto-Bismol.

Everything we suggested was met with a constraint as to why it couldn't be achieved, often by former members of a team that produced similar software for the other bank rather than the one that had produced the software we were reviewing. Every time we asked to talk to users to help us understand their jobs, we were told their jobs may be eliminated through making this software more efficient. The whole first day we felt like we'd been dropped into the movie *Office Space.*

That evening, I met with the project sponsor and said, "Can you tell me what's going on here? What can we do to help you instead of stressing everyone out?" We scrapped the entire agenda that evening, and reframed our discussions around participation.

Instead of becoming part of the uncertainty of the merger, we asked members of both teams to break into small groups and present their software systems to the smaller group, including our team. We shifted into facilitating and sketching, and asked the group members to drive the dialogue. One of us facilitated the dialogue and made occasional comments to reinforce a point, while another captured the best practices in sketches and notes, and a third team member took screen shots and video.

I ended the session by telling our sponsor I was leaving the firm to join Obama for America. It all worked out well, but I never felt so good getting on a plane.

Now, let me tell you about the time I had the usability test participant show up stoned.

She was afraid of yellow. . .

Russ Unger

Coauthor of Designing the Conversation

Russ is a user experience designer and researcher in the Chicago area.

I was asked to give a keynote for a conference. Once I got past the rush of the ask, I settled into the nervousness that comes from being a closing act. I had gone through all the rituals necessary to prepare me for the presentation, so when it came time to get onstage, I was as ready as I was going to be.

I gave my talk, and it went as well as it could have; the audience seemed to enjoy the content and they felt very engaged from my perspective.

Upon completion of the Q&A, I thanked everyone for their time, and they applauded. I set to tearing down my gear and putting things away.

Something felt off.

There was silence. Deafening silence.

I looked up, and everyone in the room was still in their seats. They were waiting.

I looked around and found the conference organizers nowhere to be found, and no one was nearby that I could throw under a bus to handle this growing awkwardness that I was feeling.

I said, "That's it—thanks! You can go now!" and disappeared again back to my tearing down as people started to get up and make their way out of the room.

The moral is that you should not only practice and prepare for a presentation, scope out the space you'll be speaking in, and familiarize yourself with the equipment, but also understand what's going to happen before and after your time on stage. The audience was waiting on closing comments and instructions that I had no information about and was not prepared to give, which left me feeling like I'd let them down. That's the last thing you want to feel when you're a presenter, much less the closing keynote for the day.

Laura Creekmore

President, Creek Content

Laura Creekmore is president of Creek Content, a content strategy and information architecture consultancy focusing in health care, higher education, and other complex fields.

I go to several conferences that really appreciate "thought piece" presentations. You know, the ones where you're sharing a new way of thinking about something, but you don't really offer a concrete takeaway. The mindset is the takeaway. Last year I came up with (I'm still convinced) a brilliant idea for this kind of presentation, and I pitched it to a conference I'd never attended before. They accepted.

I got a room full of folks to my talk, but five minutes in, I could tell they weren't with me. It wasn't that they didn't understand what I was saying—I think they did—but they wanted something different out of it. After I finished [early, mercifully], every single question was about practical application.

It was the worst time I've ever had presenting, and my biggest disappointment was the sense that I'd disappointed the audience.

Will I do another thought piece in the future? You bet—but I'll also choose the forum for it very carefully. Now I think much more carefully about audience expectations when I'm planning a presentation.

Aaron Irizarry

Experience Design Lead

Aaron Irizarry is an experience design lead at HP where he tries to improve the conversation around design on a daily basis. He also speaks on the topic of critique and design studio.

I recently put together a presentation on responsive frameworks for something at work. I was excited, I knew my content, and I was ready to save the world one user at a time.

While presenting the content I could tell that stakeholders and other product team members were starting to get the deer in the headlights look. Some folks on the team were getting it, but they were mostly designers. The effort was delayed due to a lack of understanding and buy-in, which meant that a couple of months of research, education, evangelizing, and design/code effort were wasted.

After the presentation I realized that even though I was comfortable with the content, I needed to inquire about team understanding and make sure that I presented the content in a form that allowed the team to understand it and understand its value.

David Farkas

Lead Interaction Designer

David Farkas is a Philadelphia-based interaction designer who works on a variety of business systems and consumer goods.

My method of preparation has served me pretty well. That said, I learned the importance of it the hard way. I was working with a client I've built a relationship with over the course of a year and was presenting updated design concepts to them. I didn't print the outline of my slides, nor did I rehearse. In my mind, we were reviewing updates from the previous meeting and everyone was familiar with my work.

I walked into the room and saw two familiar faces out of about a dozen. Pushing the panic aside, I went into the updates—no priming of the reason for the meeting, and no description of the work done to date. Not surprisingly, I was immediately derailed and asked what was being shown, its purpose, and the process to get there. What I expected to be a half-hour review became a two-hour working session. And all because I didn't set the expectations and look to see who my audience was.

Never again will I fly by the seat of my pants and, more importantly, never again will I expect my audience to know what I'm talking about. Treat every presentation like it's someone's first. And never get lazy in organizing your thoughts. Always be prepared for a conversation to be derailed.

Dale Sande

Another UI Guy

Dale Sande is a maker of things, a general do-gooder, and a vanquisher of evil. He loves the HTMLs, the CSSs (really Sass), the JavaScripts, the Rubies, and the Rails.

Confidence in your presentation is paramount. I had a lucky streak where back-to-back presentations were wildly successful and I felt I could do no wrong. Then I was invited to a local mobile meetup. Right from the beginning I felt the whole thing go sideways.

From the introductions of the group I quickly discerned that the majority of attendees were amateur developers and mobile hobbyists. Because of the education level of the room, much of the material I was going to talk about was going to be hard to communicate. If the audience wasn't able to relate to the material or see an opportunity for direct application, then all would be lost. And sure enough, it wasn't long before things really started to fall apart.

My topic was to address issues with UI development with emphasis on speed and performance. Early into the discussion, people were already disengaged. I knew I was in trouble when not even five minutes into the presentation I was asked, "Why should I care? After all, they'll just keep making the Internet faster."

I was trapped. No matter what reasoning I gave to dispel the myth that we can build crappy apps and hardware manufacturers and telecoms will simply make the Internet faster, this guy would not budge. Then the iOS versus Android versus Windows Mobile and even RIM slandering began to fly. My initial discussion on abstract best practices for managing a high-performance UI degraded quickly into a dogmatic us-against-them free-for-all.

Ironically, the week before I gave this exact same presentation to another group and the engagement was so positive that I spoke for four hours. At one point I was given a bar stool to sit on and a mic. It was awesome. But this was not the case with this group. I had to muster all my strength to keep going despite the stubborn opinions of some in the room who wanted to derail the conversation and interject their opinions, not to mention the two people I noticed who were completely asleep.

I stood tall, read through the material, flipped through the slides, and finished the presentation professionally. And then got the hell out of there.

The lesson learned from this experience is that when doing this kind of stuff, you have to expect the unexpected. This was my first really bad experience. Sure I had some sour presentations leading up to that one, but this one was by far the worst. I learned not to engage the trolls in the audience, much as a comedian will ultimately fail when engaging a heckler. Simply smile, acknowledge their opinion, and move on.

Presentations are tough. Audiences are tough. But I assure you that what's going on in your own head is much worse than what anyone in the audience is thinking.

Ross Belmont

Chief Experience Designer

Ross Belmont gave up a life of code to build the design practice at Appiphony, a Chicago-based consultancy focused on Salesforce.com apps.

A client asked us to build a relatively simple survey application used initially on an iPad, and perhaps in other ways down the road. They brought us in after firing the agency that did their brand work from the project, after seeing some wireframes and not being impressed. We sensed a multidevice deployment in the future and prototyped a responsive design that deviated markedly from their initial wireframes. The pitch was a disaster: They said they were "at a loss" and asked why we moved away from the work that had already been done. My boss was able to backpedal, and we built what they had in mind. Now, we don't try to blow people's minds during pitches, and instead carefully frame up our design concepts as solutions to problems raised by clients during prior discussions. They are almost a nonevent if we build enough trust in the first few meetings.

Nick Disabato

Interaction Designer

Nick Disabato is a freelance interaction designer and publisher from Chicago.

At one presentation in front of a packed auditorium full of really fancy, influential people that was being streamed live on the Internet, I knocked an open bottle of water into my laptop's keyboard. Now I keep the bottle closed, or carry it. In one case, I put a beer bottle in my back pocket, walked around for a few minutes, and pulled the bottle out and took a sip. Nobody was expecting the bottle to be there, and it generated a few laughs!

The exception, not the rule

No facilitator sets out to create a horror story; horror stories happen. While no amount of preparation, planning, and practice can help you avoid disasters, your work beforehand will help you keep tabs on the things you can control and hopefully allow you to dedicate your energy to doing your best to solve the challenge in front of you.

Sometimes you simply won't be able to do anything about the mess you're caught in the middle of. Do your best to remember that all things pass, and like these horror stories from experts in the field, it will likely be much funnier later when you're able to reflect on it.

Index

WATCH
READ
CREATE

Unlimited online access to all Peachpit, Adobe Press, Apple Training, and New Riders videos and books, as well as content from other leading publishers including: O'Reilly Media, Focal Press, Sams, Que, Total Training, John Wiley & Sons, Course Technology PTR, Class on Demand, VTC, and more.

No time commitment or contract required! Sign up for one month or a year.
All for $19.99 a month

SIGN UP TODAY
peachpit.com/creativeedge

creative
edge